Warrior • 114

African American Soldier in the Civil War

USCT 1862–66

Mark Lardas · Illustrated by Peter Dennis

First published in Great Britain in 2006 by Osprey Publishing,
Midland House, West Way, Botley, Oxford OX2 0PH, UK
443 Park Avenue South, New York, NY 10016, USA
E-mail: info@ospreypublishing.com

A CIP catalog record for this book is available from the British Library

ISBN-13: 978 1 84603 092 5

Page layout by: Mark Holt
Index by Alison Worthington
Typeset in Helvetica Neue and ITC New Baskerville
Originated by PPS Grasmere, Leeds, UK
Printed in China through Worldprint

08 09 10 11 12   11 10 9 8 7 6 5 4 3 2

FOR A CATALOG OF ALL BOOKS PUBLISHED BY OSPREY MILITARY AND
AVIATION PLEASE CONTACT:

NORTH AMERICA
Osprey Direct, c/o Random House Distribution Center, 400 Hahn Road,
Westminster, MD 21157
E-mail: info@ospreydirect.com

ALL OTHER REGIONS
Osprey Direct UK, P.O. Box 140 Wellingborough, Northants, NN8 2FA, UK
E-mail: info@ospreydirect.co.uk

www.ospreypublishing.com

Author's acknowledgments

I would like to thank Paul J. Matthews of the Buffalo Soldiers
National Museum in Houston, TX, and Michael Knight of the
National Archives, for assisting me in the collection of some
of the illustrations that appear in this book. I also wish to
thank my father-in-law, William Potter, for helping obtain
illustrations and source material. The illustrations marked
"Potter Collection" were supplied by him.

Author's note

The quotations in this book are rendered accurately from
the contemporary sources. I have preserved the epithets,
grammatical errors, and language used; the quotes do not
reflect my own views, but rather those of the participants.

Many of the quotations in this book come from *Born in
Slavery: Slave Narratives from the Federal Writers' Project,
1936–1938*. This collection contains interviews of 2,300
former slaves who were still living in the late 1930s. The
collection is available online (see the references). Quotations
from these interviews are cited in the following format:
[interviewee's last name] Narrative (e.g. Cole Narrative).

Author's dedication

To my new sister-in-law, Christala Lardas. Welcome to the
family.

Artist's note

Readers may care to note that prints of the original
paintings from which the color plates in this book were
prepared are available for private sale. All reproduction
copyright whatsoever is retained by the Publishers. All
inquiries should be addressed to:

Peter Dennis
The Park
Mansfield
Nottinghamshire
NG18 2AT
UK

The Publishers regret that they can enter into no
correspondence upon this matter.

Glossary

contraband	a runaway slave owned by a master in rebellion against the United States; the name is due to such slaves being declared "contraband of war."
Corps d'Afrique	name applied to early black regiments raised by the Union in Louisiana
Free Men of Color	free blacks, especially propertied blacks, in Louisiana
Native Guard	name applied to first three black Union regiments in Louisiana (these were the only black regiments raised with black officers)
NCO	non-commissioned officer (sergeants and corporals)
USCC	United States Colored Cavalry
USCHA	United States Colored Heavy Artillery
USCI	United States Colored Infantry
USCLA	United States Colored Light Artillery
USCT	United States Colored Troops
USV	United States Army Volunteers

CONTENTS

AFRICAN AMERICAN SOLDIER IN THE CIVIL WAR: USCT 1862-66

INTRODUCTION

In 1861 when President Lincoln issued a call for 75,000 troops I engaged myself for the great Civil War, the War of the Rebellion. The United States was not taking Negro troops.

(Alexander H. Newton [a free black living in New York City],
Out of the Briars.)

For the Civil War's first two years slavery was the elephant in the room – an unavoidable object whose presence was denied. The Union government was determined to show that the war was not about slavery. It was about preserving the union or states' rights – although both sides knew that slavery was the only states' right that could rupture the union. The Civil War started as a white man's war. The Union refused to enlist blacks for fear of further alienating the rebelling states, and losing the states that had not seceded but were unsupportive of abolition.

To win European support for the Confederacy, the South employed "show units" of unofficial state militia regiments in New Orleans and Memphis. These had no official duties except to march in parades when foreign newspapermen were present. These men had to provide their own weapons and equipment, apart from when the South abandoned New Orleans and gave the blacks worn-out muskets to cover the retreat of the white units. With this unusual exception, the Confederacy refused to allow participation by freed blacks, and was not yet sufficiently desperate for manpower to arm slaves. African Americans could serve only as auxiliaries: servants, teamsters, or cooks.

On May 26, 1861, the Union general Benjamin Butler, then commanding Fort Monroe, Virginia, refused to return three runaway slaves to their owner – a colonel in the Confederate Army. Butler held that runaway slaves belonging to owners in rebellion against the United States were "contraband of war." Like any property providing military advantage they could be seized. Congress approved of his logic: it ratified Butler's position on August 6, 1861, passing the First Confiscation Act, which directed the armed forces to confiscate property employed in the service of the rebellion – including slaves.

This was aimed more at harming rebellious slave-owners than emancipating slaves. Yet large numbers of "contrabands" collected wherever the Union established outposts in the Confederate states. The Army was barred from using these blacks. Congress passed the Militia

Act on July 17, 1862, allowing the Army to hire contrabands as laborers, to be paid one ration a day, and $10 per month, $3 worth of which should be provided as clothing. African Americans could be hired only as laborers – not as soldiers.

Some generals attempted to recruit blacks to fill shortages in their numbers. One Union commander, Gen David Hunter, unofficially raised a regiment of runaway slaves in South Carolina in April 1862. Ordered to disband the regiment, he refused to do so, and was relieved. Benjamin Butler was more successful in September 1862. Commanding Union forces in New Orleans, Butler raised three regiments of black troops. He cleverly used the fiction that he was recommissioning and expanding the regiment of Free Men of Color that had served in the Confederate Army.

In reality, fewer than 10 percent of the members of the Confederate regiment reenlisted in the Union Native Guard regiments raised by Butler. Despite claims that all the recruits were freemen, half were slaves, most runaways, when they enlisted. In one regiment, a company was raised from slaves owned by a free black, Francis Dumas – who received a captain's commission.

Butler commissioned the 1st Native Guard Regiment on September 27, 1862. A few days earlier, on September 22, 1862, Lincoln issued the preliminary Emancipation Proclamation. This only freed slaves in regions "in rebellion against the United States." As with the Confiscation Act, it was primarily intended to harm the Confederacy. The Emancipation Proclamation also ended any chance of European intervention – unless the Confederacy similarly eliminated slavery. Additionally, the casualties of the Peninsular Campaign were hard to justify in a war merely to "preserve the union."

Shifting the war aim towards emancipation, as well as union, removed barriers to African Americans serving in the Army. Butler kept his regiments. To the west, the State of Kansas was also in the process of raising a regiment of African American troops – in this case acknowledged

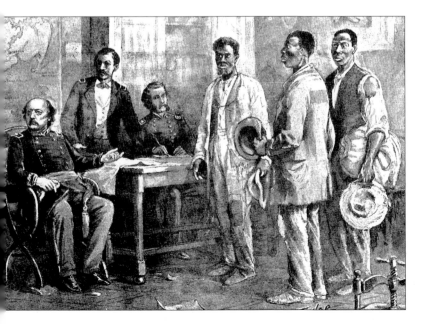

Gen Benjamin Butler (seated) declared these runaways to be contraband of war, when their master, a Confederate officer, tried to claim them. Butler later raised the first three African American regiments using this premise. (Author's collection)

runaways from Missouri. That fall, Hunter's unofficial regiment was reconstituted as the 1st South Carolina (Colored) Regiment, commanded by Col Thomas W. Higginson, an abolitionist Unitarian minister who had supported John Brown and the anti-slavery Jayhawkers in Kansas before the Civil War. By January 1, 1863, when the Emancipation Proclamation took effect, additional African American regiments were being raised in North and South Carolina, and Louisiana. The New England states, Massachusetts foremost among them, were clamoring for permission to raise African American regiments.

The common soldiers' opposition to fighting alongside African Americans faded. Many objected to African Americans, but the casualty lists at Fredericksburg convinced other white soldiers of the virtue in the "racially tolerant" view that:

> The right to be killt I'll divide with him,
> And give him the bigger half!
> (William Wells Brown, *The Negro in the American Rebellion*)

Conscription further weakened opposition to African American soldiers. When the Federal Conscription Act took effect in July 1863, riots protesting against the Act took place in some Northern cities. Often led by white Irish immigrants, the rioters turned their resentment at being conscripted to liberate slaves – viewed as potential competitors for their jobs – against blacks in those cities. In New York City African Americans were hunted down by mobs, and a black orphanage was burned down.

As William Wells Brown recorded in his history of African American participation in the Civil War, most people seriously expected that the "niggers won't fight." But fight they did. Sometimes, as at Port Hudson and Fort Wagner, they lost. At other early actions, most notably at Honey Springs and bloody Milliken's Bend, they won. The Union Army, hungry for men, realized that the experiment was successful, and expanded it. Black men could fill conscription quotas as well as whites. States were willing to persuade, pay, or compel blacks to join. By the end of 1863 over 50,000 blacks had joined the Army. By the war's end 178,975 blacks had enlisted.

Blacks were segregated, serving in African American regiments, not as part of white formations. With the exception of Butler's Native Guard regiments, the officers appointed to African American regiments were white. Owing to white prejudice, only a handful of blacks received commissions in the new regiments, most in 1865 or 1866.

Members of African American units faced death if captured. Some of the first prisoners captured from such a regiment were executed: the African Americans were summarily executed as slaves in rebellion, and the whites tried and hanged them for inciting slave rebellion. One of the commanders in the West, Ulysses S. Grant, hearing what had happened promised to execute one Confederate prisoner for every member of an African American unit executed for rebellion. The official killing stopped, but these soldiers still risked unofficial acts of murder, massacre, and maltreatment if they fell into Confederate hands.

African American regiments were initially given state names. Federal, not state authorities, raised the regiments with Southern state names. Few Union states were eager to claim African American regiments. The effort

THE (FORT) MONROE DOCTRINE.

Can't come back nohow massa
Dis chile's contraban

Come back you black rascal!

was federalized; a Bureau for Colored Troops was created, and the African American regiments became the United States Colored Troops (USCT). The 1st US Colored Infantry Regiment (USCI – United States Colored Infantry) came into existence on the eve of Gettysburg. By the beginning of 1864 the existing state regiments – except for those from Massachusetts and Connecticut, states with abolitionist governors and state legislatures – were renumbered under the Federal system. For example, the 1st South Carolina (Colored) became the 33rd Regiment, USCT.

By the war's end, the USCT regiments earned the respect of those they fought with – and against. They proved to be among the best units in the Union Army: dogged in defense, relentless in attack, and disciplined when on garrison duties.

CHRONOLOGY

1860

December 20   South Carolina secedes from the United States.

1861

February 4   Confederacy formed; joined initially by North and South Carolina, Georgia, Florida, Alabama, Mississippi, Louisiana, and Texas.

April 12   Fort Sumter fired upon by Confederate forces.

April 15   President Lincoln declares a state of insurrection and sends out a call for volunteers.

May 26   Gen Benjamin Butler refuses to return three runaway slaves to their Virginian owners, claiming they are "contraband of war."

August 6   First Confiscation Act passed.

1862

July 17   Militia Act first authorizes Army to enlist African American laborers at a rate of one ration a day and $7/month, plus $3/month in clothing.

August   Kansas Senator Jim Lane begins recruiting the 1st Regiment of Kansas Volunteers (Colored).

September 2   Black Brigade of Cincinnati organized as unarmed labor force.

September 22 Lincoln issues the Emancipation Proclamation to take effect January 1, 1863.

In one of the first encounters between the 1st South Carolina (Colored) and the enemy, Confederate troops released bloodhounds used to track and control runaway slaves against them. Instead of running from the dogs as their former masters expected, the Union soldiers used bayoneted rifles to settle the score. (Author's collection)

| September 27 | Benjamin Butler swears the 1st Regiment of the Louisiana Native Guard into service. |

1863

January 1	Emancipation Proclamation takes effect.
May 22	Bureau for Colored Troops established by General Order No 143.
May 27	1st and 3rd Louisiana Native Guard regiments (Corps d'Afrique) lead assault on Port Hudson, LA.
June 7	Battle of Milliken's Bend.
July 4	Union wins Gettysburg and Vicksburg surrenders.
July 17	Battle of Honey Springs.
July 18	54th Massachusetts attacks Fort Wagner, Charleston, South Carolina.

1864

February 20	Battle of Olustee.
April 12	Fort Pillow Massacre.
June	Congress authorizes "all persons of color who were free" in April 1861 to be paid same wage as white soldiers.
June 15	Siege of Petersburg begins. Twenty-two USCT regiments participate.
July 30	Battle of the Crater.
August 22	Atlanta falls.
September 29	Chapin's Farm, Virginia. Thirteen USCT soldiers win Medal of Honor.
November 8	Lincoln reelected.
December 3	25th Army Corps Organized – only corps almost exclusively comprised of USCT units.

1865

March 3	Enrollment Act authorizes Army to pay all African American soldiers the same wage as whites, retroactive to January 1, 1864.
April 2	Siege of Petersburg ends.
April 3	Richmond falls to the Union.
April 9	Lee surrenders at Appomattox.
May 15	63rd USCT regiment fights at Palmetto Ranch, Texas, the last major action of the Civil War.

ENLISTMENT

Hart's Island, NY, 1864

Madam – I seat myself at this time as an opportunity affords itself to me to drop you a few lines in way of a communication, to inform you that I am well; and I hope when this comes to hand that it may find you all the same. My object in writing is to inform you that I have enlisted in the army of the United States for one year, but having faith and confidence in my Father above, I live in hopes to get back home once more, when I expect to find my work and old customers waiting for their old whitewasher and house-cleaner to resume his old station. As time is short, and business so brisk, I will have to come to a close. I now remain yours most obediently,

Isaac Stokeley,
NY, Colored Regt
(Post, *Soldiers' Letters*)

Alexander Newton, who had unsuccessfully attempted to enlist in 1861, fled New York City after the July 1863 draft riots. In December, living in New Haven, Connecticut, he achieved his goal of engaging himself for the great Civil War. As he wrote in his memoirs, "On the 18th of December, 1863, I enlisted Twenty-Ninth Regiment of the Connecticut Volunteers, as a private."

Isaac Stokeley and Alexander Newton were among 178,975 blacks enlisting in the United States Army during the American Civil War. In some ways they were atypical. Less than one-sixth of the blacks that joined the Army were – like these men – residents of free states. The rest came from slave states. The majority of the 99,337 enlisted from states in rebellion against the United States were from Louisiana, Mississippi, and Tennessee.

The Civil War was nearly two years old before the Army changed its policy to permit blacks to enlist. African Americans throughout Union-controlled areas celebrated when they could finally join. (Author's collection)

Newton was also born a freeman. Most enlistees were slaves – runaways, or slaves from Union states who joined to become free. Stokeley was probably a runaway slave when he enlisted. The rolls of the 31st USCI – the only Colored Regiment raised at Hart's Island – show an Isaac Small and an Isaac Still, but no Isaac Stokeley. Stokeley was probably an assumed last name, to provide a runaway slave a defense against slave-catchers. If so, Small or Still reclaimed his real name when he enlisted, but wrote to a former employer in the name by which he was known to her.

In the free states a black could enlist at a recruiting station. Generally these were located in large cities, or smaller towns with black communities, such as New Bedford, Massachusetts, or Oberlin, Ohio. James H. Gooding, a seaman from New Bedford, enlisted in a hometown company raised for the 54th Massachusetts (Colored) by Capt William Grace, a white New Bedford merchant. Black communities and abolitionist organizations funneled potential recruits to northern rendezvous, where regiments were forming. In some cases, they ran the Underground Railroad in reverse, taking former runaways in Canada back to the United States.

In early 1863, reaching a recruiting rendezvous could be a challenge – especially in regions with a strong anti-African American element like New York City, or southern Ohio and Indiana. Travel arrangements were often made secretly, with sympathetic whites purchasing the tickets. Even in abolitionist strongholds, like Massachusetts, individual white opposition made enlisting difficult. When the 54th Massachusetts was being organized, one Army recruiter in Boston refused to enlist African Americans.

In slave states, including loyal slave states, African American regiments went to the blacks to find recruits. One of the first duties of an officer assigned to a new African American regiment was leading recruiting parties. Joseph M. Califf, a captain in the 7th USCI, later wrote of these duties in his *Record of the Services of the Seventh Regiment,* "The usual method of proceeding was, upon reaching a designated point, to occupy the most desirable public building ... found vacant, and with this as a rendezvous, small parties were sent into the surrounding country, visiting each plantation within a radius of twenty or thirty miles."

By 1863 the Union was hungry for soldiers. African Americans who joined were promised their freedom and pay. The response was enthusiastic. Califf related: "The laborer in the field would throw down his hoe or quit his plow and march away with the guard, leaving his late master looking after him in speechless amazement."

Nor were slaves slow to take advantage of the opportunity offered. In some cases, sympathetic owners encouraged their slaves to join. John Eubanks of Kentucky got his owner's permission, as he narrated: "He say, 'enlist in the army, but

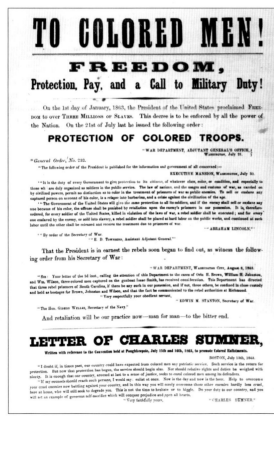

One of many recruitment posters encouraging blacks to join the Union Army in 1863. (National Archives)

don't run off.'" Eubanks then "walked 35 miles from Glasgow to Bowling Green, to the enlisting place. On the way I meet up with two boys. They run away from Kentucky, and we go together."

Eubanks's master was unusual. Most wanted to keep their slaves. That did not prevent slaves from enlisting, even in loyal states. William Emmons, also a slave in Kentucky, said that he:

> left and joined the Army when I was 18. Forty of us from the plantation around Carlisle went at the same time... Three white fellows we knowed came riding up and says, "Where you darkies going?" We told him we was going to war, and they tried to make us go back to the plantation. We told them we'd kill them sure enough, if they kept meddling with us. They got scared and left us alone. (Emmons Narrative)

Slaves in areas of the Confederacy not controlled by the Union also enlisted. Their first challenge was reaching Union lines. John Young, born a slave in Arkansas, was one such enlistee:

> I run off from home in Drew County [Arkansas]. Five or six of us run off to Pine Bluff. We heard that if we could get with the Yankees we'd be freed, so we run off to Pine Bluff and got with some Yankee soldiers... Then we went to Little Rock, and I joined the 57th Colored Infantry. (Young Narrative)

Escaping was risky. One runaway, Barney Stone, recalled his escape:

> One day when I learned that the Northern troops were very close to our plantation, I ran away and hid in a culvert, but was found, and would have been shot, had the Yankee troops not scattered them [his pursuers] and that saved me. I joined that Union Army.
> (Stone Narrative)

Not all blacks were as eager – or willing – to join up, as Henry H. Buttler showed in the tale of his escape:

> In 1863, Mr. Sullivan transported about 40 of us slaves to Arkansas, locating us on a farm near Pine Bluff, so we would not be taken by the Federal soldiers. They had a chance to escape, and go to the free states. I think I was the only one that deserted Mr. Sullivan. I went to Federal Headquarters at Fort Smith, Arkansas, and was received into the Army. (Buttler Narrative)

James Ayers, a recruiter from Illinois, recounted in his diary experiences with reluctant recruits:

> I have often been told by them when trying to coax them to enlist, "why," they say, "I don't want to be a soldier."
> "Well," say I, "you will be made free men just as soon as you enlist."
> "Oh sir," say some, "I would rather be a slave all my days than go to war. I can't shoot, nor I don't want to shoot anybody. I can't fight."

"Well," say I, "we can soon learn you."
"Yes massa, but I have a wife."
"So have we," say I, "and don't you think our wives are dear to us as yours are to you?"
"Well, Master, I ain't fit for a soldier, anyhow."
"Well, what's the matter?"
"Oh sir, I's corrupted," meaning ruptured, or "got rheumatism" or pain in the back, or pneumonia, or arm bent tooth ache or some excuse...

Peter Bruner, a private in the 12th Regiment, United States Colored Heavy Artillery (USCHA), told of encountering reluctant slaves on a recruiting mission in *A Slave's Adventures Towards Freedom*:

We came to two or three large plantations. There were a great many colored people and as soon as they saw us they ran. We started after them and succeeded in capturing about 15 of the men. We started with our men and camped out at the foot of a hill and commenced to get supper when we were fired on by the rebels. This scared the recruits so bad we had gotten that they ran again. After this skirmish with the rebels, we coming out victorious, we caught our recruits and took them to camp. They cried, some of them, like babies and we had to let them go.

The first experience a recruit might undergo was a physical. Thomas J. Morgan, who commanded an African American regiment, described this process in his *Reminiscences of Service*:

The first thing to be done was to examine the men. A room was prepared, and I and my clerk took our stations at a table. One by one the recruits came before us *a la Eden, sans* the fig leaves, and were subjected to a careful medical examination, those who were in any way physically disqualified being rejected. Many bore the wounds and bruises of the slave-driver's lash, and many were unfit for duty by reason of some form of disease to which human flesh is heir. In the course of a few weeks, however, we had a thousand able-bodied, stalwart men.

Where black enlistment was voluntary – mainly in Military Districts containing the loyal slave states (Maryland, Delaware, Kentucky, Missouri, and parts of Tennessee) – potential recruits disqualified due to disabilities often persisted in trying to join. These Districts created invalid regiments, made up of troops incapable of field service but capable of garrison duties to utilize these willing, but physically disqualified men.

Other Military Districts, notably those containing Kansas, Louisiana, and the Carolinas, conscripted African Americans for the Army, especially from the pools of contrabands in those regions. Additionally, African Americans in the Northern states were liable to conscription along with whites, and African Americans could serve as substitutes for whites who were drafted. Hunter's Regiment (as it was referred to by Thomas Higginson in *Army Life in a Black Regiment*) consisted almost exclusively of conscripts. There, the enlistment physical yielded different results.

Esther Hill Hawks, a volunteer doctor who served in both North and South Carolina, reported the results of one such parade in *A Woman Doctor's Civil War*:

All of the men who came in for examination were either hopelessly lame and come hobbling along with (new) sticks cut for the purpose not many rods from Camp or they have some mysterious disease which has baffled the skills of all doctors way back to "ole massa's time" and the amount of suffering such men will bear and the stubbornness with which they persist in shamming disease, in order to escape "soldiering" is truly wonderful! The examinations are very ludicrous.

Men who passed inspection – whether volunteers or conscripts – then enlisted. They signed papers committing them to serve in the United States Army for a fixed period. Those joining when the regiment was forming typically enlisted for three years. Those, like Stokeley, enlisting after the training period ended, or in the field, committed to one year's service.

Enrolling a name was straightforward for the Northern free blacks, but could be a challenge for slaves, many of whom had been known by a single name up to that point. Henry Romeyn, an officer in the 14th USCT, related one such encounter in a memoir written after the war:

A man had passed the scrutiny of the medical officers and was asked his name.

Conscription applied to blacks in the Civil War as well as whites. Some blacks became substitutes for white draftees; others, like these reluctant recruits, had to be impressed into service. (Author's collection)

The first steps to joining the
army were an examination
by a recruiting officer followed
by a physical examination.
(Author's collection)

"Dick," was the reply.
"But every soldier, white or black, has two names; what other one
do you want?"
"Don't want none – one name enough for me."
"You *must* have one. Some of these men take their mother's name,
some take their old master's. Do you want to be called by your old
master's name?"
"No sah, I don't. *I's had enough of ole masser.*" (Romeyn, "With
Colored Troops in the Army of the Cumberland")

Many runaways refused to take their master's name. Omelia Thoma[s]
told an interviewer: "My father said he was really George LeGrande. Bu[t]
after he enlisted in the War he went by the name of George Grant[.]
There was one of the officers by that name, and he took it too" (Thoma[s]
Narrative). Generals Butler, Banks, Thomas, and Weitzel frequentl[y]
found themselves similarly honored.

TRAINING

*The first attempt to "form company" was a crucial test of the faith of the
new officer. No uniform clothing had been issued, and many of the recruits
had scarcely rags enough to hide their nakedness. I confess that I was
staggered, almost appalled, at the thought of the self-imposed task.*

(Henry Romeyn, on taking charge of a company in the 14th
USCI Regiment)

Less promising material for soldiers than the newly recruited Africa[n]
American troops was hard to find in Civil War America. Most slave[s]
were unfamiliar with firearms. It was illegal for slaves to use them. Mos[t]
were uneducated. It was a felony to teach slaves to read and write[.]
"Keep books and guns out of slave hands if you want to keep the[m]

laves," was how Joe Higgerson, a slave who joined the Union Army, explained ante-bellum policy in his narrative. Even in free states, the ability of black freemen to own guns was highly restricted. Most literate Northern blacks were self-educated.

"The enlisted men of my regiment were mostly slaves from the plantations of those counties of Maryland and Virginia which lie east of the Chesapeake Bay," stated George R. Sherman, a white officer in the 7th USCI, in "The Negro as a Soldier." "These recruits came to us ignorant of anything outside their own plantation world." Ignorant slaves were slaves less likely to hold disruptive opinions.

The black soldiers of the USCT possessed two things that allowed them to overcome this handicap: experienced officers and a willingness – by the private soldier – to learn and work hard.

White regiments elected their company officers. Of USCT regiments, only two of the three Louisiana Native Guard regiments raised by Gen Butler had officers assigned that way. The rest were appointed. The first regiments had white officers appointed by state governors who wished to see the experiment of using black troops succeed. Later the officers, almost all white, were appointed by the Army, and had to pass an examination prior to receiving a commission.

At a minimum these men had seen combat, and were experienced in military life. White officers could gain promotion as field officers in an African American regiment – major, lieutenant-colonel, or colonel. Non-commissioned officers, even privates, could receive the shoulder strap of a company officer. This drew numerous volunteers. The Army could be (and was) choosy about giving promotion. Candidates had to demonstrate that they possessed the skills to operate their command – whether a company or a regiment – and that they were motivated to become officers in an African American regiment for reasons beyond the financial gain and additional status this potentially easy route to promotion brought.

To ensure an adequate supply of competent officers, supporters of using black troops created an officer-training academy in Philadelphia. Enlisted whites seeking a commission in the African American regiments could obtain leave to attend this preparatory academy prior to a board examination. The experiment was so successful that it was imitated in the Spanish–American War.

The recruits were also highly motivated to learn to be soldiers. For ex-slaves the payment for success would be freedom. For Northern freemen, it was the opportunity to gain respect, and the rights of citizenship. George Sherman stated, "They are quick to learn the manual of arms, and the evolutions of the army drill. In these they took great pride and pleasure, and when well uniformed their appearance was always good."

The first task was organizing the thousand men in a regiment. Recruits were broken into 100-man companies. Often the companies, identified by letter, were organized along with the regiment, the

Learning to handle firearms transformed slaves into soldiers. Blacks and their white officers knew that someone who could shoot was too dangerous to keep as a slave. (Library of Congress, Prints and Photographs Division)

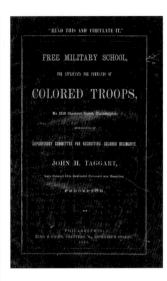

When a shortage of qualified officers for the African American regiments developed, a training school was established in Philadelphia. (Library of Congress, Prints and Photographs Division)

first men enlisting being assigned to Company A, with the final hundred assigned to Company K. (There was no Company J.) Thomas Morgan "assigned them to companies according to height, putting men of nearly the same height together. When the regiment was full, the four center companies were composed of tall men, the flanking companies of men of medium size, while the little men were sandwiched between. The effect was excellent... It was not uncommon to have strangers who saw it on parade for the first time, declare the men were all of the one size."

For members of the USCT training meant drill, drill, and drill followed by more drill. Jacob Bruner, an officer in the 9th Louisiana Volunteers (Colored), wrote to his wife in May 1863: "We have about one hundred men recruited. We drill twice each day. I am detailed to drill a squad tomorrow. They learn very fast and I have no doubt they will make as rapid progress as white soldiers."

Units that could fire their muskets more quickly and more accurately than their opponents, units that could maneuver more quickly than their opponents, won. Achieving proficiency meant practicing the steps to load, aim, and fire a musket until it became instinctive. It meant practicing marching and changing formation until such actions became as natural as breathing. So officers constantly drilled their men. Henry V. Freeman described training his regiment, the 12th USCI, in "A Colored Brigade in the Campaign and Battle of Nashville":

> Drill was incessant. The whole regiment was at first an extremely awkward squad. But some of the men proved apt pupils. The more intelligent were soon able to assist their more awkward comrades. In what seems now a remarkably short space of time the men were making good progress in company and regimental drill, and were a fair way to become soldiers, so far as drill and a knowledge of camp duties could make them such.

In *On the Altar of Freedom* James Gooding wrote of the evolution of his unit, the 54th Massachusetts (Colored), and the pride that the men showed in their accomplishment:

> During the past week things have assumed a more military shape than before, owing to the fine state of the weather, permitting outdoor drilling. Since the men have been in camp the drilling has been conducted in empty barracks, until the past week. It is quite enlivening to see squads of men going through their evolutions.

Competition developed between the various units in a regiment. Lt Col Nelson Viall, of the 14th Rhode Island Heavy Artillery (Colored), noted:

> It was gratifying to observe when a new company was mustered into service a strong feeling to emulate and excel the companies previously organized. In company movements they took especial pride. It was no uncommon occurrence where several companies were drilling together, for one company to rest awhile and observe closely the movements of the others. (Chenery, *The Fourteenth Regiment*)

Even the most skeptical officers in the Union Army conceded after watching African American regiments that had finished training, "Men who can handle their arms as these do, will fight." Gen George H. Thomas, a Virginian who initially doubted the utility of African American troops, after watching Thomas Morgan's regiment, told Morgan that he "never saw a regiment go through the manual of arms as well as this one."

Part of the training process was developing non-commissioned officers – sergeants and corporals. While white NCOs were used initially, blacks quickly replaced most. An infantry regiment had 55 sergeants and 86 corporals. An artillery or cavalry regiment required 65 sergeants and 102 corporals.

NCOs were chosen for literacy, leadership, intelligence, and appearance. Senior sergeants – sergeant majors, the company first sergeants, and the quartermaster and provost sergeants – all had to handle paperwork. That demanded literacy – or a very good memory.

Literate recruits could be found in Northern regiments. Many ex-slaves could read and write. Black newspapers published in the North and informal networks formed before the war taught black runaways to read. Becoming literate was seen as a first step towards being truly free. The 54th Massachusetts and 29th Connecticut recruited the cream of the North's blacks. A shopkeeper in civilian life, Alexander Newton became quartermaster sergeant of the 29th Connecticut because he already possessed the skills for the job.

Among regiments raised in slave states finding literate individuals was more difficult. Henry Romeyn, with the 14th USCI raised in Kentucky, picked someone from outside that state. "I had one man – free born – from north of the Ohio who could read and write and made him my first sergeant."

Thomas Higginson, of the 1st South Carolina (Colored), was able to find slaves among the runaways who enlisted and had secretly taught themselves to read and write. Of Prince Rivers, who eventually became the regiment's sergeant major, he wrote in *Army Life in a Black Regiment*:

There is not a white officer in this regiment who has more administrative ability, or more absolute authority over his men; they

Camp William Penn outside Philadelphia was one of the biggest training camps for African American troops. Here one regiment (probably the 127th USCI) stands in mass formation. (National Archives)

do not love him, but his mere presence has controlling power over them. He writes well enough to prepare for me a daily report of his duties in the camp; if his education reached a higher point, I see no reason why he should not command the Army of the Potomac.

Illiteracy was not always a bar to promotion, especially in regimen[t] raised in the South. Higginson promoted the initially illiterate Robe[rt] Sutton to corporal, later writing of the man, "If not in all respects th[e] ablest, he was the wisest man in our ranks... Not yet grounded in th[e] spelling-book, his modes of thought were clear, lucid, and accurate."

For many blacks, especially those enlisted from slavery, it was the fir[st] opportunity they had ever had to assume a responsible position [of] leadership. While some fell short, most thrived in their positions. Thom[as] Morgan wrote of his NCOs, "They proved very efficient, and had the w[ar] continued two years longer, many of them would have been competent [as] commissioned officers." It was a remarkable concession in a bigoted ag[e.]

Former slaves had to adjust to the concept of fellow blacks havin[g] authority over them. "'He needn't try to play the white man over me[,]' was the protest of a soldier against his corporal the other day," stated C[ol.] Higginson in his memoirs. "To counteract this I have often to remin[d]

The Presentation of Colors was a solemn ritual that marked the entry of a regiment into service. Here the 22nd USCI receives its colors in a public ceremony. (Potter Collection)

them that they do not obey the[ir] officers because they are white, b[ut] because they are their officers; an[d] guard duty is an admirable school f[or] this, because they readily understan[d] that the sergeant or corporal of th[e] guard has for the time more authori[ty] than any commissioned officer who [is] not on duty."

During training, the regiment w[as] presented with its regimental color[s.] These were two flags – the nation[al] colors and a regimental standa[rd] unique to the unit. The symbol of th[e] regiment, the colors were used to ra[lly] the regiment on the battlefiel[d.] Capturing an enemy's colors was a[n] ultimate honor for a regiment an[d] losing its own was an ultimate disgrac[e.] To protect the colors each regime[nt]

ppointed a color guard – two sergeants who held the colors and eight corporals who defended them. Joseph Califf described the formal ceremony in which the colors were presented to the 7th USCI:

At dress-parade on this day the regimental colors were brought out for the first time, and a color-sergeant and color guard selected. In doing it, Col. Shaw called the non-commissioned officers of the regiment together and stated to them the danger as well as the honor of the position to be filled, and then called for volunteers. Nearly all stepped to the front, and a selection was made from among those volunteering.

When training had been completed – a process that took 60 to 90 days – the regiment was ready to march to war.

APPEARANCE AND DRESS

A colored sentinel was marching on his beat in the streets of Norfolk, VA, when a white man, passing by, shouldered him insolently off the sidewalk, into the street. The soldier, on recovering himself called out, – "White man, halt!"
The white man, Southerner like, went straight on. The sentinel brought his musket to a ready, cocked it, and hailed again, – "White man, HALT, or I'll fire!"
The white man, hearing shoot in the tone, halted, and faced about.
"White man," continued the sentry peremptorily, "come here!"
He did so.
"White man," said the soldier again, "Me no care one cent about this particular Cuffee, but white man bound to respect this uniform (striking his breast). White man, move on!" (Brown)

This drawing, widely reproduced in the late 19th century, expresses the transformation in status that the uniform provided. Even an ex-slave, under the color of his authority, could order the actions of the Army's commanding general. (Author's collection)

The USCT wore uniforms and carried equipment identical to that of the rest of the Union Army. That gave the uniform value to the blacks that wore them. In their view it transformed a slave into an object of dignity: an American soldier.

The first attempts to create African American regiments were accompanied by attempts to clothe these units in special uniforms. Susie King Taylor, a runaway black slave who married a sergeant in the 1st South Carolina (later the 33rd USCI), wrote in *Reminiscences of my Life in Camp* of the uniforms given to Hunter's Regiment, "The first suits worn by the boys were red coats and pants, which they disliked very much, for they said, 'The rebels see us, miles away.'" When the 54th Massachusetts was being organized, some well-meaning white supporters advocated clothing the regiment in canary yellow and scarlet, as they believed that blacks – like children – would be attracted to bright colors.

Most black soldiers procured a studio photo of themselves in uniform, often with weapon in hand. (Library of Congress, Prints and Photographs Division)

The dignity of men like James Gooding was never challenged by such comic-opera costumes. By the beginning of 1863 the Federal government had massive stockpiles of issue uniforms and equipment for any number of new regiments. It was also disinclined to spend extra money on brightly colored African American uniforms. Hunter's Regiment – to its enlisted personnel's relief – surrendered its red pantaloons and jackets for the sky blue and navy blue of the rest of the Army, including other African American regiments. Jacob Bruner wrote to his wife, "As fast as we get them we clothe them from head to foot in precisely the same uniform that 'our boys' wear, give them tents, rations and Blankets and they are highly pleased and hardly know themselves" (Bruner Letters).

The men serving in the USCT viewed their uniforms as an indication that they were accepted as soldiers: men, not chattels. They treated their uniform and equipment with reverence. Often, one of the first places visited after their initial pay muster was a photographer's studio – for permanent record of their status as United States soldiers.

Given a choice, black troops showed a preference for the most formal uniform combinations. The Native Guard (later Corps d'Afrique) regiments organized with black officers opted for the dressier infantry frock coat over the four-button sack coat, and the crowned Hardee (or Hancock) hat over the kepi or forage cap. The appearance was more professional and less civilian than that preferred by white troops. Thomas Morgan related that his men "took great pride in appearing on parade with arms burnished, belts polished, shoes blacked, clothes brushed, in full regulation uniform, including white gloves."

One of the war's ironies was that the black troops, despised as they were by both sides, ended up with some of the best equipment and uniforms of any group of troops in the war. It was not due to a regard for black troops. By the time that the Union Army was recruiting blacks, inferior equipment in Army warehouses, such as the 1816 smoothbore muskets or Mexican American surplus equipment, had already been distributed to existing units. Early war shortages had been satisfied; the crooked contractors and those producing the shoddiest goods had been identified and weeded out. By 1863 uniforms and equipment purchased were worth keeping and of good quality. While it was happenstance that black troops got good equipment – there was simply very little shoddy equipment in the warehouses – the troops took it as a message that they were valued. They returned value for value – fighting harder than anyone expected them to fight.

Years after the war, the uniform and equipment remained a fond memory. "The uniform I wore was blue with brass buttons; a blue cap lined with red flannel, black leather boots, and a blue cap. I rode a bay color horse – fact everybody in Company K had bay color horses," Albert Jones, a private in Company K of the 1st US Colored Cavalry, told an interviewer 60 years after the war ended (Jones Narrative). Some soldiers kept their uniform as a touchstone. Arthur Boone, who joined the 9th Louisiana after it became the 63rd USCI, kept his gun and uniforms after the war. His son J. F. Boone related, "My oldest brother kept that gun and them blue uniforms with the brass buttons" (Boone Narrative).

The brass buttons held particular fascination for the black soldier. A former slave related that during her day of liberation:

When the colored troops come in they were playing:

Don't you see the lightning?
Don't you hear the thunder?
It isn't the lightning.
It isn't the thunder.
But the buttons on the Negro uniforms!

Frederick Douglass predicted as much in a recruiting speech given on July 6, 1863: "Once let the black man get upon his person the brass letters U.S.; let him get an eagle on his button, and a musket on his shoulder, and bullets in his pocket, and there is no power on the earth or under the earth which can deny that he has earned the right of citizenship in the United States."

African American troops received the same kit as the white soldiers: a wool blanket and a rubberized blanket or poncho, and a haversack, knapsack, and canteen. They either used the same wall or Sibley tents as their white counterparts, or were issued half a dog tent – identical to regular army issue. As with the uniforms, the quality was excellent. For an ex-slave, who previously owned nothing – even the clothes on his back – the army kit represented wealth beyond dreams.

John McMurray, an officer in the 5th USCI, wrote in his memoirs of Charles Hubbard, a private in his company:

He could not bear to see anything go to waste, but seemed to think it his duty to gather up all of the stuff the other boys didn't want or gotten through with, especially in the clothing line... He would always have two pairs of trousers, always two shirts, and usually three; never less than two blouses, his knapsack full and bulging out and two woolen blankets strapped on top; in addition to all this, a frying pan, coffee pot, tin cup, and various other cooking utensils tied to his load here and there with strings.

McMurray, a white raised in comfortable circumstances, found Hubbard's behavior eccentric, but Hubbard must have found

Company E of the 104th USCI pose outside their barracks in their best uniforms shortly before being discharged. The quality of uniforms issued to black soldiers is obvious in this photograph. (Library of Congress, Prints and Photographs Division)

21

This anonymous drummer boy was one of the many slaves in Louisiana who escaped bondage and joined the USCT to secure his freedom. (National Archives)

McMurray's casual attitude towards property – things of value that you could actually keep – equally odd.

The USCT was equally fortunate when it came to weapons. American Indian regiments had to make do with inferior firearms. Many white regiments soldiered through the war with smoothbore muskets, some dating back to the War of 1812. Other units had castoffs from European armies. As with uniforms, by the time the Union began raising African American regiments, the armories were empty of the worst rifles.

William Gladstone documented that African American infantry regiments intended for front-line duties were virtually uniformly armed with either the 1861 Springfield or the 1853 Enfield – first-line rifled muskets, and the best muzzle-loading rifles issued during the war. Infantry regiments intended to guard supply lines or prisoners, or hunt guerrillas, might be issued second-class weapons, like the Lorenz rifle from Austria. Garrison troops, especially the heavy artillery regiments, were issued third-class rifles, such as the .69-cal. Prussian or Austrian rifles. In all cases he found that African American units fought with functional rifles, appropriate to the service provided by a unit, no smoothbores.

If black soldiers were proud of their uniforms, they were enthusiastic about their weapons. For most, it was the first time that they were allowed to use weapons. Even those like James Gooding, a whaler who used both firearms and harpoons, took satisfaction in their weapons. Gooding wrote home about the experience, "Yesterday the men received their new arms. We are supplied with the Enfield rifle, made in 1853, so you may suppose they intend us to make good use of them; and I doubt not, that if the opportunity presents itself, they *will* be made good use of."

As with much of their army life, the black recruits' enthusiasm meant they mastered their tools quickly. Col Higginson wrote, "One captain said to me to-day, 'I have this afternoon taught my men to load-in nine times, and they do it better than we did it in my former company in three months.'"

CONDITIONS OF SERVICE AND DAILY LIFE

During my temporary absence as brigade inspector my own company refused to answer their names when I inspected them, thinking I had left the company and was trying to make them take seven dollars per month... I know of no white regiment that would have remained in the service thirteen months as my company has, without any pay, that would have given us less trouble.

(Capt Thomas W. Fry, 14th Rhode Island Heavy Artillery [Colored], relating a "mutiny" over pay. [Chenery])

Black troops experienced equality in uniforms and weapons because of circumstance, not policy. They were issued with good equipment when it was easier and cheaper for the Army to do so. But black troops suffered discrimination, especially when it came to pay, rations, and work assigned

James Gooding had a genuinely American response to his unequal pay – he wrote a letter to the President, petitioning for redress of grievances. The letter is preserved today in the National Archives.
(National Archives)

Pay was the most egregious discrimination that blacks experienced. The first black regiments raised, including the Rhode Island regiment whose officer is quoted, were promised the same pay as their white counterparts. Congress took 18 months to fulfill that promise. The first law authorizing the Army to pay African Americans was the Militia Act, passed by Congress in July 1862. It set the pay for all African American employees of the Army at laborers' rates: one ration per day, and $10 per month, of which $3 was to be in clothing.

The intention was to see that contrabands hired by the Army as laborers were paid reasonably. However, it meant that no African American recruit, regardless of rank, could be paid more than $7 per month. In January 1863, when the 54th Massachusetts was raised, a white private received $13 per month, and a white sergeant major $21 per month.

The reaction of African American soldiers who enlisted after being promised pay equal to whites can be imagined. Alexander Newton remembered in his memoirs, "When we were told by him [the Paymaster] that we could receive only $7 per month each, for our services our spirits fell. So I, together with the rest of my comrades, was really disgusted with this failure on the part of the Government to give us a decent compensation for our work as soldiers."

James Gooding recorded the reaction of the 54th Massachusetts to the first pay parade in which they were to accept this pay cut: "He [Col Littlefield] then said, 'all who wish to take the *ten* dollars per month, raise your right hand,' and I am glad to say not one man in the whole regiment lifted a hand."

Another black soldier in the 54th Massachusetts wrote home about his feelings of humiliation:

We have fought like men; we have worked like men; we have been ready at every call of duty, and thus proved ourselves to be men: but still we are refused the thirteen dollars per month. Oh what a shame to be treated thus! ... Sir, the Fifty-fourth and Fifty-fifth Regiments would sooner consent to fight for the whole three years, gratis, than to put ourselves on the same footing of contrabands... We enlisted

It took two years of steadfast service before African American troops received pay equality, but most received equal pay, plus the difference in what they were owed, before their final pay muster. However this was not always the case and some troops never received their back pay. (Author's collection)

as Massachusetts Volunteers, and we will not surrender that proud position, come what may. (Redkey, *A Grand Army of Black Men*)

Only Congress could fix this problem after the Attorney-General ruled that it was illegal to pay African American soldiers – freemen or former slaves – more than $7 per month. While unequal pay was recognized as an injustice, Congress's efforts to correct it were blocked by the Peace Democrats, who wanted to discourage slaves from joining the Army. By starving the Army of soldiers – including African Americans – the Peace Democrats felt they could force the war to end.

Blacks continued to join, and to fight, regardless. Newton recorded "We quieted our passions and went to work like good soldiers." Higginson related:

In my regiment the men ... seemed to make it a matter of honor to do their part, even if the Government proved a defaulter; but one third of them, including the best men in the regiment, quietly refused to take a dollar's pay, at the reduced price. "We'se give our soldiering to de Government, Colonel," they said, "but we won't despise ourselves so much for to take the seven dollars." They even made a contemptuous ballad, of which I once caught a snatch.

> "Ten dollar a month!
> Three of that for clothing
> Go to Washington
> Fight for Lincoln's daughter!"

"Lincoln's daughter" stood for the Goddess of Liberty. They would be true to her, but they would not take the half-pay.

Eventually, gradually, the African American soldier received justice. Shamed by the performance of units like the 54th and 55th Massachusetts, Congress granted equal pay to freedmen in July 1864. The Peace Democrats blocked increasing the pay of troops enlisted as slaves or runaways above the level of laborers' wages, although they provided the same military service as their free brethren. Finally, in March 1865 a new

Congress, purged of Peace Democrats by the 1864 election, gave all African American troops equal pay retroactive to January 1, 1864. The 20,000 slaves who enlisted in 1863 lost pay for that year's service, and those who died before the pay rise was voted never received the retroactive pay.

Even then, few of the former slaves received the bounty for enlisting. If a man had been a slave in April 1861, he was not entitled to the general enlistment bounty when he joined. Slaves owned by loyal whites – such as those recruited in Kentucky and Maryland – saw their bounty go to their former owner, as compensation for the loss of their property. In the 7th USCI, the officers went to the Secretary of War and secured a special $100 bounty for the majority of their men ineligible for other bounties, but few regiments had such dedicated officers.

Army rations were plentiful and nutritious, if dull. Unfortunately, because it was easy to shuffle spoiled rations to African American regiments, they received more than their share of bad food. (Library of Congress, Prints and Photographs Division)

Those soldiers who managed to get a bounty, and collect their accumulated pay, often ended up with nothing. Many African American soldiers put their savings in the Freedman's Savings Bank. It collapsed in 1874, taking two-thirds of the money saved by the African American veterans.

A second problem faced by African American troops was poor rations. Like white troops, African American soldiers received:

> twelve ounces of pork or bacon, or one pound and four ounces of salt or fresh beef; eighteen ounces of soft bread or flour, or twelve ounces of hard bread, or one pound and four ounces of corn-meal; and to every 100 rations, fifteen pounds of beans or peas, or ten pounds of rice or hominy; ten pounds of green coffee or eight pounds of roasted (or roasted and ground) coffee, or one pound and eight ounces of tea; fifteen pounds of sugar; four quarts of vinegar; one pound and four ounces of andamantine or star candles; four pounds of soap; three pounds and twelve ounces of salt, and four ounces of pepper. (Official Records)

The problem was the quality of the ration received. Food was perishable. John Billings, a white soldier who wrote of life in the Army, observed that this led to "... quantities of stale beef, or salt horse, served out and rusty, unwholesome pork" and "petrified bread honeycombed with bugs and maggots." Billings noted that "Unwholesome rations were not the rule, they were the exception" (Billings, *Hard Tack and Coffee*). Bad food was neither universal nor Army policy. It was not limited to black troops: white units also received poor-quality rations on occasion. However, African American regiments were the most recent units added to the Army and the ones least likely to have their NCOs working with the commissariat. Add a belief that quality did not matter for blacks, and African American regiments often became the home for such rations.

While many USCT officers rejected substandard food sent to their regiments, the 32nd USCI was one regiment ill served by its officers.

Benjamin Williams, a private in that regiment, bitterly wrote, "All the rations that are condemned by the white troops are sent to our regiment. You should see the hard tack we have to eat. They are moldy and musty and full of worms, not fit for a dog to eat, and the rice and beans and peas are musty, and the salt horse (the salt beef, I mean) is so salt that after it is cooked we can't eat it" (Redkey).

As additional African American regiments joined and were brigaded together, the problem eased. Most rations were of good quality. A division or brigade rarely got more than a regiment's worth of spoiled food. Once African American regiments were brigaded together, it was harder for brigade quartermasters outside the African American brigades to shuffle spoiled food to black regiments. Indifferent, disengaged, or uncaring officers willing to accept spoiled rations existed among the African American regiments, but there was less scope to exploit this.

African American troops also got a disproportionate share of fatigue duties, the messy, but necessary tasks associated with maintaining an army: gathering firewood, digging and filling in "sinks" (as latrines were called), clearing stables, building roads, cleaning equipment, preparing entrenchments. Fatigue duties were the unavoidable hard, dirty, dull, and utterly vital activities. African American regiments had no objection to doing their share of a camp's fatigues, but in many camps white units escaped fatigue duties by having their commanders (generally senior to the officers in black regiments) assign all fatigues to the African American regiments.

White units rationalized passing fatigues to African American units on the grounds that these tasks were work appropriately assigned to ex-slaves, but as George W. Williams in his *History of the Negro Troops* observed:

> Fatigue duty had a very unhappy effect upon these troops. They had enlisted to fight, not to be hewers of wood. They were proud of their uniforms, and desired above all things to be led against their ancient and inveterate foes. It was natural, therefore, that they should feel disappointed, and in some instances doubt the Government that had broken faith with them.

Excessive fatigue duties hurt readiness. "The large details required for picket and fatigue on the fort leave little opportunity for drills," noted William H. Chenery, a lieutenant in the 14th Rhode Island Heavy Artillery (Colored).

As Sherman prepared to march against Atlanta, the African American regiments were detailed to fortify Chattanooga. "This incessant labor interfered sadly with our drill, and at one time all drill was suspended by orders from headquarters," remembered Thomas Morgan, "There seemed little prospect of our being ordered to the field, and as time wore on and arrangements began in earnest for the new campaign against Atlanta, we began to grow impatient of work, and anxious for opportunity for drill and preparations for field service."

Fatigues allowed Sherman, who mistrusted the fighting abilities of African American troops, to march without African American regiments because they were unready for field service, circular reasoning that gave Sherman what he wanted: an all-white force to take to Atlanta.

Finally, Lorenzo Thomas, the Adjutant-General of the United States Army, issued Order No 21, in June 1864. It directed that "... the practice which has hitherto prevailed, no doubt from necessity, of requiring these [African American] troops to perform most of the labor on fortifications and the labor and fatigue duties of permanent stations and camps will cease, and they will only be required to take their fair share of fatigue duty with the white troops" (Official Records). The order came too late for Morgan's 14th USCI to participate in Sherman's Atlanta campaign, but permitted them to prepare for field service in the latter half of 1864.

Even after Order No 21 African American regiments played supporting roles. Most of the 145 black regiments raised by the United States Army were assigned post or garrison duty. Only 60 saw action on the battlefield, including regiments protecting lines of communication against guerrillas and raids. Only a quarter were assigned to offensive field service.

The duties these rear-echelon regiments performed were vital, but dull. The 14th Rhode Island Heavy Artillery (Colored), like many heavy artillery regiments, was assigned the task of providing security along the mouth of the Mississippi River. Lt Chenery wrote of the battalion garrisoning Ship Island, to monitor shipping to and from New Orleans: "Among the duties appertaining to the garrison were those of boarding all inward bound vessels and examining the papers of the captains. This duty necessitated the keeping of a boat's crew constantly on the lookout, and made it less monotonous for the garrison, as every steamer and sailing craft was signaled to heave to by firing a blank cartridge from the water batteries." The opportunity to burn gunpowder and participate in examining a ship made the artillerymen feel more like soldiers and less like laborers.

Another group of this regiment stationed at English Turn suffered from boredom and disease. Capt Joshua M. Addeman wrote in "Reminiscences of Two Years with the Colored Troops," "Our men were

Lorenzo Thomas, the Adjutant-General of the United States Army, was given the task of raising the USCT regiments. Here he is pictured (top left) in Louisiana, addressing blacks on the responsibilities of freedom. (Library of Congress, Prints and Photographs Division)

dropping off from a species of putrid sore throat, which was very prevalent. The soil was so full of moisture that we had to use the levee for a burial ground. Elsewhere, a grave dug two feet deep would rapidly fill with water."

Later, when his company was transferred to the healthier Plaquemine they encountered a different goad. "The surrounding country was infected with guerrilla bands, and in the jail were a number of rebel prisoners who had been captured in recent raids. The latter received from the town's people very gratifying evidences of sympathy." It was a sympathy the occupied town lacked for its black garrison. "As we marched through the streets of the village to the site of our camp," recalled Addeman, "the scowling looks of white spectators sufficiently indicated their sentiments and especially their wrath at being guarded by 'niggers.'"

Occupation duty could be dangerous, but it was more typically tedious. When time hung heavy officers and men found ways to make it pass. Jim Spikes, who served in the 55th USCI, told an interviewer, "When we was in Fort Pickens I remember they had a poll parrot – some of the officers had trained it to say, 'Corporal of the guard, Jim Spikes, post no. 1. Sometimes I would draw my gun like I was going to shoot, and the poll parrot would say, 'Jim, don't you shoot me'" (Spikes Narrative).

African American troops were used to guard prisoners, a task which pleased freed slaves but not their former masters. "At Point Lookout the guards were all negroes; and it is well known that they improved every opportunity to testify their peculiar regard for their former masters," wrote John Whipple, a white guard at Elmira, NY. "They would shoot down a rebel on the slightest provocation, or infringement of orders. A prisoner said to me: 'If we got only one foot over the line of our camp we could not get back again too quick;' for the guard had rather shoot them than not" (Post).

Whipple added, "For the first nights after their arrival here [Elmira] the night-patrol was composed of negroes; and the universal exclamation [from the Confederate prisoners] was 'Let white men guard us, and we shall be satisfied. We do not want them damned niggers over us.'" In *Point Lookout Album* John Jacob Omenhausser, held a prisoner at Point Lookout, described the black troops' attitude towards this duty by quoting the African American guards: "The bottom rail's on top now."

African American troops were often assigned the task of escorting supplies through guerrilla-infested or contested territory. Peter Bruner described how he and a small party from his regiment conducted one such journey from Bowling Green to Nashville, Tennessee, to guard a thousand head of cattle:

Everything went well with us until we arrived at Franklin, Tennessee. After we had passed into Franklin the next night we went into camp, everything began to go wrong. The food gave out and the rebels fired in on us. The rebels had three men to our one but they did not get any of our men or cattle. All of this occurred after night. We managed the next day to go to the mill to get some flour and when we came back we made it up with water and put it on a board and held it up before the fire to bake it. That evening we found a hog that had five little pigs just about three days old and cleaned them and made soup of them. About that time that the soup was done the rebels fired in on us and made us go and forget all about our pig soup. So after this we did not have any more trouble until we reached Nashville with all of our cattle safe.

African American troops were often used to guard lines of communication against attack. Here soldiers from the 1st Louisiana Native Guard provide security for a railroad line. (Library of Congress, Prints and Photographs Division)

Securing the captured portions of the Confederacy was a vital task frequently assigned to African American regiments, to free veteran regiments to mount offensives against the Confederate Army. The vital, but dreary, task of hunting down guerrillas was left to newly formed, but less experienced African American troops. Lt Anson S. Hemingway, of the 70th USCT, wrote home about one action:

There has been a party of guerrillas prowling about here, stealing horses and mules from the leased plantations. A scouting party was sent out from here in which was a company of colored cavalry commanded by the colonel of a colored regiment. After marching some distance they came upon the party of whom they were in pursuit. There were seventeen prisoners captured and shot by the colored soldiers. (Post)

The camp of the 10th USCI, stockaded huts with dog tent roofs were typical of camp accommodations for infantry, both white and African American. (Library of Congress, Prints and Photographs Division)

Whether African American troops occupied territory, guarded prisoners, fought guerrillas, or escorted supplies, the work they did was as vital to ultimate Union victory as fighting on the battlefield.

Life in camp

Most USCT soldiers were assigned to permanent camps. Camp life followed a routine similar to that of white soldiers. Often, the first task was to build the camp. Henry Romeyn described the process in the Army of the Cumberland, in Tennessee:

> Shelter tents were put up on log sides four feet high, slabs were procured for building a dispensary, two log cabins about 14x20, and covered by shakes split from trees cut from the camp ground were erected, and material for bedding was found in the broom-sedge of an old field a mile away.

Army of the Potomac quarters, as described by Joseph Califf, were similar:

> The tents first issued were of the Sibley pattern, but these were soon replaced by the "A" or common tent. These were raised upon a stockade of rails or timber which was plastered with mud. The chimneys were made of sticks, laid up cob-house fashion, and treated to a coating of the same material, and surmounted by a barrel. But all the care that could be bestowed on these habitations failed to make them really comfortable, and after every rain the plastering process had to be repeated... [Then] the usual routine of camp duties began. Company or skirmish drill in the morning, and battalion drill in the afternoon, varied by an occasional brigade drill or target practice. Besides the ordinary camp-guard we furnished a picket detail, and fatigue details to the engineering officers for making slashings [brush used in fortifications], cutting timber, building earthworks, etc.

Even on service, continued drill and training was vital to readiness. Meals served at camp were based on the rations described earlier. In the 1st South Carolina food quality was not a problem. According to Susie King Taylor:

> We had fresh beef once in a while and we would have soup, and the vegetables they put in them were dried and pressed... Sometimes the men would have what we called slap-jacks. This was flour, made into bread and spread thin on the bottom of the mess-pan to cook. Each man had one of them with a pint of tea, for his supper, or a pint of tea, and five or six hard tacks.

One key responsibility in camp was mounting guard. Thomas Morgan wrote that:

> Colored soldiers acted as pickets, and no citizen was allowed to pass our lines, either into the village or out, without a proper permit. Thus many proud southern slaveholders found themselves

marched through streets guarded by those who three months earlier had been slaves. The negroes often laughed over these changed relationships as they sat around their camp fires, or chatted together while off duty, but it was very rare that any southerner had reason to complain of any unkind or uncivil treatment from a colored soldier.

Night guard duty was tedious, despite occasional excitements. "During the war some of us had to always stay up nights and watch for the rebels," explained Albert Jones. "Plenty of nights I had watch, but the rebels never attacked us when I was on" (Jones Narrative). As James Gooding put it, "If a person were to ask me what I saw South, I should tell him stinkweed, sand, rattlesnakes and alligators. To tell the honest truth, our boys on picket look sharper for snakes than they do for rebels." Charles H. Anderson, a private in the 122nd USCI, had a livelier night on picket duty: "It was pitch dark, and I heard something coming through the brushes, and I thought, 'Let 'em come, whoever it is.' I got my bayonet all ready and waited. I's getting sorta nervous, and pretty soon the bushes opened, and what do you think it was? A great big old hog!" (Anderson Narrative)

Soldiers in garrison had leisure, after dinner and before taps, or lights out. Thomas Higginson described a typical evening in his regiment:

Beside some of these fires the men are cleaning their guns or rehearsing their drill, – beside others, smoking in silence their very scanty supply of the beloved tobacco, – beside others, telling stories and shouting with laughter over the broadest mimicry, in which they excel, and in which the officers come in for a full share... Then there are quieter prayer-meetings, with pious invocations and slow psalms, "deaconed out" from memory by the leader, two lines at a time, in a sort of wailing chant. Elsewhere, there are conversations around fires, with a woman for queen of the circle... By another fire there is an actual dance... And yonder is a stump-orator perched on his barrel, pouring out his exhortations to fidelity in war and in religion.

African American troops participated in the assault on Port Hudson and later formed much of its garrison. This is one of the companies based there. (National Archives)

Officers in African American regiments tried to avoid punishments reminiscent of their men's lives as slaves on the plantation. Riding the sawbuck – having a miscreant sit on an elevated rail – was a popular alternative used for minor offenses. (Author's collection)

One pastime that absorbed African American troops, especially former slaves, was learning. For runaways in the Union Army, learning to read and write and mastering arithmetic were a pleasure and a way of defying their former owners. Esther Hill Hawks wrote, "they are all eager to go to school, books being the one thing denied them, they have a frantic desire to get possession of them; yesterday a couple of half-grown boys, came to see if I would teach them to read. The book they brought was a fine vol. of Virgil which they had rescued from the wreck of the Public Library!"

Most commanders took advantage of this desire to learn. Thomas Morgan "established in every company a regular school, teaching the men to read and write, and taking great pains to cultivate in them self-respect and all manly qualities." Henry Romeyn noted that "Men went to fatigue duty with spelling books or alphabet cards in the pockets of their blouses, to be studied in the intervals of labor, and a book tucked in the belt of the sentry as he walked his beat, was a very common sight." The illiteracy that Romeyn complained of when his regiment formed quickly disappeared, as his men conquered ignorance as surely as they fought tyranny.

Barney Stone profited by these efforts. "When I went into the army I could not read or write. The white soldiers took an interest in me, and taught me to write and read, and when the war was over I could write a very good letter" (Stone Narrative). It formed the basis for his formal education once the war ended.

Maintaining discipline in African American regiments could be tricky. Overly harsh punishments demoralized the soldiers. Thomas Higginson observed:

> In dealing out punishments, we had carefully to avoid all that was brutal and arbitrary, all that savored of the overseer. Any such dealing found them obstinate and contemptuous. A system of light punishments, rigidly administered according to the prescribed military forms, had more weight with them than any amount of angry severity. To make them feel as remote as possible from the plantation, this was essential. By adhering to this, and constantly appealing to their pride as soldiers and their sense of duty, we were able to maintain a high standard of discipline – so, at least, the inspecting officers said – and to get rid, almost entirely, of the more degrading class of punishments.

On campaign

For the USCT regiments that served on campaign life was at times rougher and better than it was in a permanent camp. Except in a long, formal siege – such as the eight months before Petersburg – a soldier was limited to the comforts he could carry on his back. A night's camp would be primitive, especially in cold weather, as Peter Bruner described in his memoirs: "We camped out in little dog tents all winter. The tents were just large enough for two men to stay in, they were about four feet high. Often when we awakened in the morning we would be covered with snow. It blew into the tents and our blankets would be frozen to the ground so we could hardly get up."

In a siege, at least the tents could be heated. On the lines at Petersburg, Alexander Newton was also living in a dog tent, but "We dug

Private, 54th Massachusetts, 1863

A

B

C

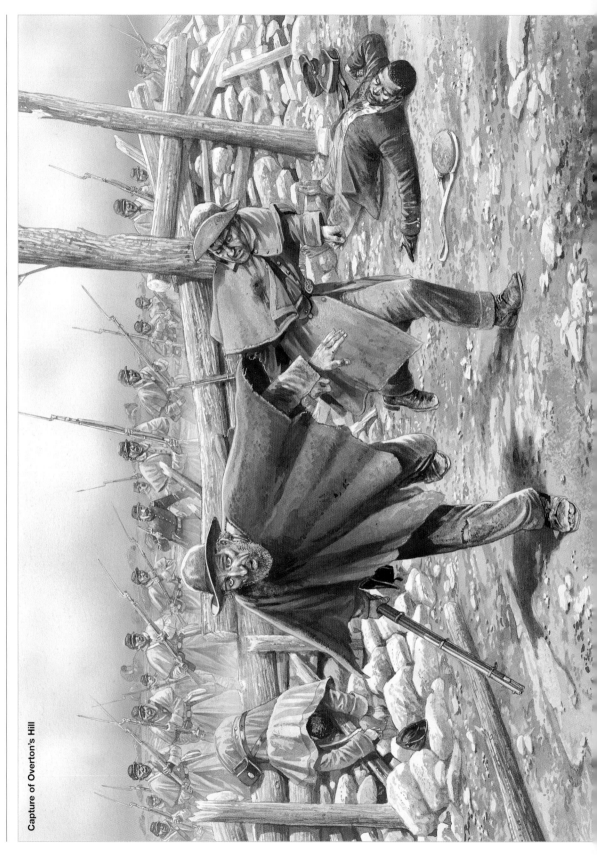

Capture of Overton's Hill

D

The battle of Honey Springs

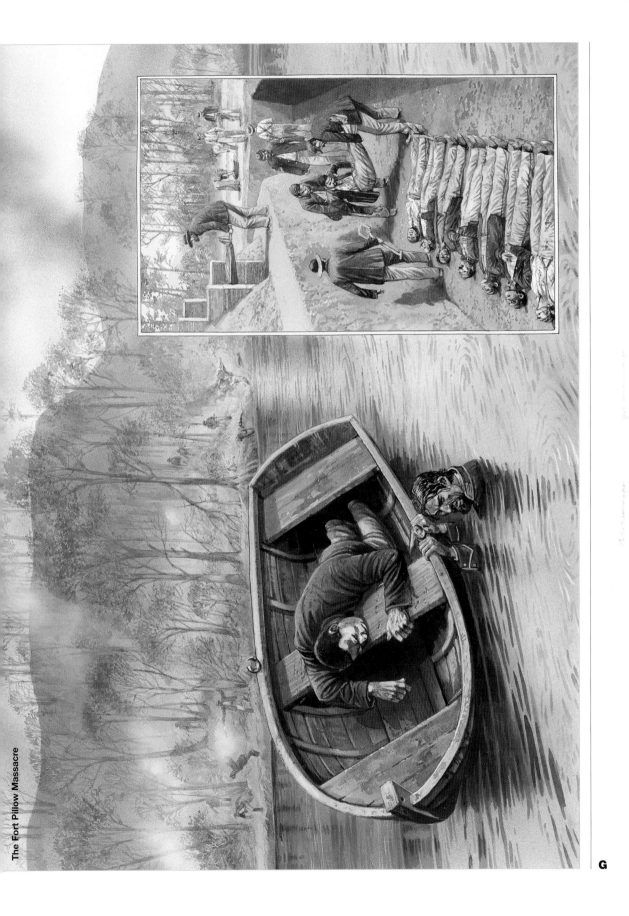

The Fort Pillow Massacre

Garrison duty: USCT sergeant major at Charleston, 1865

H

holes about two feet wide extending from within outside the tent, and placed sheet iron over these, and in these small trenches started our fires. In this way we were able to have heat within, and force the smoke outside."

Hygiene was a problem on campaign. Alexander Newton told of the battle he fought to stay clean:

We were greatly annoyed here as well as in other places with what the soldiers called greybacks, not the rebels, however; they were genuine creepers. They molested us no little. Whenever I could get off I would go to the creek and disrobe myself, and pick them out of my clothes, then wash my clothes and hang them on the bushes to dry. Then I would dress myself and feel like a king, because once again I was clean and free from these unearthly vermin.

Getting adequate food was a challenge. The marching ration was smaller than the camp ration. John Billings described it as "one pound of hard bread, three-fourths of a pound of salt pork, and one fourth of a pound of fresh meat; sugar, coffee and salt. The beans, rice soap, candles etc were not issued to the soldier on the march." Often soldiers on the march were issued three days' marching rations – 30 pieces of hard tack, and three pieces of salt pork – at its beginning. Preparing meals on the march could be difficult, as Alexander Newton related: "We had for our dinner, breakfast, and supper, half-done salt-pork, which was placed on a stick and held over a blaze to warm it; hard tack, on which one could hardly make an impression with the teeth, and sometimes coffee, if it could be gotten."

Not all campaigning units suffered from bad rations. Newton's 29th Connecticut was in a theater fought over for virtually the whole war. Foraging yielded little to eat. For the 14th USCI in Tennessee, as Henry Romeyn recounted, finding a good meal was much easier, especially as his unit was marching through the countryside during harvest season:

As soon as camp was reached a systematic supply department was put in operation. Four men worked together – one got wood, another water, a third raided the nearest corn-field, the fourth searched for something which had blood in it and could be made to go into a frying-pan which he carried on his musket. It was said that twelve roasting ears, "with the etceteras," could be eaten at one meal, but thirteen was an unlucky number and *might* make him ill.

Whether gathering food was considered foraging or plundering depended upon the officer in charge. Attitudes varied maddeningly, even within a regiment or company, as Peter Bruner discovered:

Once in a while we would go out and get a chicken and divide with our Captain but he did not care where we got them. Lieutenant Wallace would not allow the boys to take anything. He put one of the boys in the guard house for stealing a watermelon. So one day we thought we would go out and get some apples. We took a sack and got it full of apples. When I got back they took my apples and a revolver that cost twenty-five dollars and put me into the guard house.

A soldier's life was recorded on a card maintained by the regiment in which he enlisted. In this case, John Henry Chase of the 23rd USCI (Age: 21, Complexion: Dark) enlisted on February 24, 1864, and was killed in action on July 3. (National Archives)

Being on campaign, rather than in garrison, meant that a unit wa getting ready to fight the Confederates. Thomas Higginson describec the men of his regiment, "growing impatient of inaction. 'Ought tc go to work, Sir – don't believe in we lying in camp eating up the provisions.'" Work meant campaigning.

BELIEF AND BELONGING

Let me so live that when I die I shall have manners; that I shall know what to say when I see my heavenly Lord.

Let me live with the musket in one hand, and the Bible in the other – that if I die at the muzzle of the musket, die in the water, die on the land, I may know that I have the blessed Jesus in my hand, and have no fear.

I have left my wife in the land of bondage; my little ones they say every night "Where is my father?" But when I die, when the blessed morning rises, when I stand in the glory with one foot in the water and one foot on the land, then, O Lord! I shall see my wife and my little children once more.

(Prayer of the 33rd USCI, quoted by Col Thomas W. Higginson)

"STAND UP A MAN!"

When an interviewer in the 1930s asked James Spikes why he enlisted in the Union Army the ex-slave replied, "Why did I enlist? I did not know no better. They told us the war was supposed to set the darkies free. M old master did not want me to go on – course not." This reply captured the essence of the USCT soldier. He knew nothing of what he would find on the battlefield, but joined because he felt it was a way to gain hi freedom. His master, like most slave-owners, did not want his propert enlisting, but for the first time, Spikes could make his own decision abou his life. Joining was as much an act of defiance as it was a bid for freedom

For men that joined the Northern regiments, whether free black, o prewar runaway, there was another dimension to the struggle – equality James Henry Hall, a private in the 54th Massachusetts, wrote in a lette to a Northern newspaper, "We do not covet your wives nor you daughters, nor the position of political orator. All we ask is the prope enjoyment of the rights of citizenship, and a free title, an acknowledged share in our own noble birthplace" (Redkey). This wa the reason that so many men from these regiments, as well as the firs African American regiments raised in the Sea Islands, refused to tak

anything less than the same pay that whites received. James Gooding wrote, "Too many of our comrades' bones lie bleaching near the walls of Fort Wagner to subtract even one *cent* from our hard earned pay."

Northern blacks enlisted to free their Southern brethren as well as to gain civil rights. Sgt Charles W. Singer, of the 107th USCI, wrote an appeal to a Northern black newspaper urging other free blacks to join the fight, in which he stated, "I have no ambition, unless it be to break the chain and exclaim: 'Freedom to all!' I will never be satisfied so long as the meanest slave in the south had a link of chain clinging to his leg. He may be naked, but he shall not be in irons" (Redkey).

Religion was another motivation for the soldiers in the USCT. With little solace in a society that rejected them, most took comfort in the promise of an afterlife. Higginson has already shown us that many of the soldiers spent their hours in religious pursuits. The prayer opening this section was not just words to be recited – for the USCT solder it was a creed to live by. The war was a crusade.

The view of the war as a crusade was also held by many white officers that joined African American regiments. Thomas Higginson, first colonel of the 33rd USCI, had helped finance John Brown in both Kansas and Maryland. He recalled his thought upon being offered command of what was then the 1st South Carolina: "it was a vast experiment ... one on which the result of the war and the destiny of the negro race might rest... I had been an abolitionist too long, and had known and loved John Brown too well, not to feel a thrill of joy at last in finding myself in the position where he only wished to be."

Some white abolitionists behaved in a patronizing manner towards black troops under their command. David Hunter, rather than offering contrabands an opportunity to enlist, conscripted them, feeling that it was their duty – and that they had to be driven to it. This view of blacks as children, often mischievous and needing guidance, was common among the abolitionists who became officers in the USCT. It permeates many of their memoirs. The better among them soon viewed their subordinates as men, and the bonds between enlisted men and officers across racial divides were deep and very real.

In part this was due to the shared dangers. The white officers were as much at risk in battle as their black men. Capture could lead to murder for both owing to the Confederate policy of treating all those affiliated to USCI units as rebellious slaves, rather than legal combatants. Henry Freeman reported three cases that he knew of where officers in his 12th USC Regiment were murdered after surrendering. "Lieutenant W. L. Clark, captured on a train, was made to kneel down and shot in cold blood because he belonged to this colored regiment." Three other officers captured after the battle of Nashville, "were led off, under pretense of being sent to General Forrest's headquarters, and in a secluded ravine, without warning, were shot down like so many dogs. Two of them were instantly killed; the third ... left for dead, subsequently recovered to tell the story."

The blacks also suffered if captured. George Sherman, of the 7th USCI, related the fate of the African American soldiers captured along with him:

> Some were claimed as slaves by men who had never known them; others denied fuel and shelter through the winter, and sometimes water with which to quench their thirst; the sick and dying neglected or maltreated and even murdered by incompetent and fiendish surgeons; without rations for days together; shot at without the slightest reason, or only to gratify the caprice of the guards – all of which harrowing details were fully corroborated by the few emaciated wrecks that survived.

Deep bonds were formed. After a sniper killed Capt Charles Oren of the 22nd USCI, a sergeant in Oren's company wrote to his widow, stating "If my brother had been shot, it would not of hurt me any worse than it did when he was shot. He was a good officer, not only that, but he had his men at heart. I dearly loved him. Any thing I could do for him, would do it" (Washington, *Eagles on their Buttons*).

These bonds lasted after the war's end. Charles T. Trowbridge, who commanded the 33rd USCI after Higginson stepped down due to poor health, related an encounter with one of his men, Sgt Brown, two decades later in "Six Months in the Freedmen's Bureau." Trowbridge was "on a steamer returning from a trip to the sunny land of Florida by way of Port

Royal. From on the deck I saw among a gang of colored men who were loading cotton my little black hero. I hastened on shore, we recognized each other and in a moment he threw his arms around me, and the reunion was such as only old comrades can understand who have braved dangers together in days gone by."

THE SOLDIER IN BATTLE

Personally I shrink from danger, and most decidedly prefer a safe corner at my own fireside to an exposed place in the face of the enemy on the battlefield, but so strongly was I persuaded of the importance of giving colored troops a fair field and full opportunity to show of what mettle they were made, that I lost no chance of insisting upon our right to be ordered into the field.

(Lt Col Thomas J. Morgan, 14th USCI)

Were these men born brothers or did they become brothers-in-arms on the battlefield? Today we do not know. The bonds formed on the battlefield often transcended those of birth. (Library of Congress, Prints and Photographs Division)

One of the key questions whites had about black troops was their willingness to fight. Thomas Morgan's first battle convinced his superiors that, given a chance, his black soldiers would fight. Morgan wrote about Gen George Thomas's doubts, "He [Thomas] asked me one day, soon after my regiment was organized, if I thought my men would fight. I replied that they would. He said, 'they might behind breastworks.' I said that they would fight in the open field. He thought not."

But the black soldiers would not just fight, they would fight ferociously, even if half-trained. On June 7, 1863, at Milliken's Bend, a supply depot that had been converted to a training camp for African American regiments, three understrength black regiments beginning the process of learning to be soldiers were attacked by a brigade of Texas infantry. The Confederates, acting on outdated information, thought the camp was still Grant's main supply depot for the army besieging Vicksburg. Instead, they encountered black troops – the first that most Confederate soldiers would have met in battle. The resulting battle was a ferocious midnight brawl, with quarter neither asked nor given by either side fighting at the breastworks.

Capt M. M. Miller of the 9th Louisiana (African Descent) fought at the battle. Afterwards, he wrote a letter to a friend describing it:

I never more wish to hear the expression, "The niggers won't fight." Come with me, a hundred yards from where I sit, and I can show you the wounds that cover the bodies of sixteen as brave, loyal, and patriotic soldiers as ever drew a bead on a rebel.

The enemy charged us so close that we fought with our bayonets, hand-to-hand. I have six broken bayonets, to show how bravely my men fought. It was a horrible fight, the worst I was ever engaged in, not excepting Shiloh.

A boy I had cooking for me came and begged a gun when the rebels were advancing, and took his place with the company. When we retook the breastworks I found him badly wounded. A new recruit I had issued a gun to the day before the fight was

found dead with a firm grasp on his gun, the bayonet of which
was broken in three places. (Brown)

The outnumbered African American troops at Milliken's Bend
yielded before the Confederate attack, but did not break. At daybreak
with artillery support from river gunboats, they counterattacked, and
pushed the Confederates out of the camp.

The behavior at Milliken's Bend was typical of the battlefield
performance of black troops, who often proved the most reliable forces on
the battlefield. William Eliot Furness, who commanded black troops in both
the 3rd and 45th USCI regiments, observed in "The Negro as a Soldier,"
"There was no occasion in which they were smitten as a body with a panic
like the unreasoning panic of the Eleventh Corps at Chancellorsville, or
that of the army in general at the first battle of Bull Run."

Milliken's Bend was a defensive action. The blacks were fighting
behind breastworks. Many, including George Thomas, felt them capable
of that. The issue that remained was whether they could be relied upon
in an open field battle, or in an assault on a fortified position. That
question was decisively answered in May and later in July 1863, when
pioneer black regiments led assaults against fortified positions at both
Port Hudson, Louisiana, and Battery Wagner, off Charleston, South
Carolina. In both cases the support they were to have received from
white regiments came late. The 1st and 3rd Louisiana Native Guard
regiments (as they were then titled) at Port Hudson, and the 54th
Massachusetts (Colored) in Charleston Harbor, pressed the attack
anyway.

James Gooding wrote to his hometown newspaper about the attack
on Wagner.

> You may all know Fort Wagner is the Sebastopol of the rebels; but
> we went at it, over the ditch and onto the parapet through a
> deadly fire; but we could not get into the fort. We met the foe on
> the parapet of Wagner with the bayonet – we were exposed to
> murderous fire from the batteries of the fort, from our Monitors
> and our land batteries, as they did not cease firing soon enough.
> Mortal man could not stand such a fire, and the assault on
> Wagner was a failure.
> At the first charge, the 54th rushed to within twenty yards of
> the ditches, and, as might be expected of raw recruits, wavered –

but at the second advance they gained the parapet. The color bearer of the State colors was killed on the parapet. Col. Shaw seized the staff when the standard bearer fell, and in less than a minute, the Colonel fell himself.

Both assaults were crushed, but they were victories in the sense that they gave African American troops a fighting reputation. The officers leading them, Col Robert Shaw of the 54th Massachusetts and Capt André Callioux of the 1st Native Guards, were killed, becoming martyrs. Shaw, the scion of a prominent Boston family, was buried with his "niggers." This attempt to shame the white officer instead became a symbol of the bond between the officers and men. Callioux was one of the few black officers in the Union Army. William Wells Brown stated that Callioux "prided himself on being the blackest man in the Crescent City." Callioux demonstrated that blacks were capable not only of fighting, but of leading men into combat.

In an anonymous battle in the Indian Territory, an African American regiment, the 1st Kansas Infantry (Colored), fought a mixed force of Confederate Indians and white Texans in a battle at Honey Springs. In an open field, the African American regiment anchored the center of the Union line. They repulsed a cavalry charge launched by a Confederate force so contemptuous of the blacks that they attacked with damp gunpowder, anticipating that cold steel would make the ex-slaves run. Instead, in the words of Gen James G. Blunt, commanding the Union Army:

The First Kansas (Colored) particularly distinguished itself; they fought like veterans and preserved their line unbroken throughout the engagement. Their coolness and bravery I have never seen surpassed; they were in the hottest of the fight, and opposed to Texas forces twice their number, whom they completely routed. (Official Records)

The 1st and 3rd Louisiana Native Guard regiments' attack on Port Hudson on May 27, 1863, was repulsed at the parapet of the Confederate fort, but the bloody action showed that African American troops would fight. (Potter Collection)

47

The problem often proved to be less that African American troops would not fight, but rather that they did not know when not to fight. Whatever odds faced them, African American regiments took them on – to prove that they were both men and warriors. Throughout the war, African American regiments continued to make assaults against odds that most soldiers would consider foolhardy.

Sometimes their zeal swept the Confederates before them. In "Fourteen Months' Service with Colored Troops," Solon A. Carter wrote of one such assault, on June 15, 1864, during the assault on Petersburg. A brigade made up of African American regiments was sent to clear fieldwork commanding the City Point road.

> The line of battle advanced across the open field in splendid style, though the enemy's artillery had perfect range, and their practice was good.
>
> There was no giving way on any part of the line although progress through the wood was slow, owing to the undergrowth through which they were obliged to force their way.
>
> Emerging from the timber, the line charged with a rush, the enemy retreating before the furious onset, leaving one of their guns in the possession of the 22nd [African American] Regiment.
>
> General Hinks and his staff closely followed the line of battle, moving on a road, and upon reaching the work just captured, found a group of colored troops in extravagant demonstrations of delight at their victory.
>
> Addressing them, the general inquired: "What has become of the Johnnies?"
>
> "Well, sah, they jest done lit out; didn't care to make close acquaintance. Reckon they must have smelled us."

More typical was the result of the 7th USCT attack on Fort Gilmer, on the Petersburg lines. As described by Joseph Califf, the courage of the black soldiers proved unequal to the task given them by foolish superiors:

> Captain Bailey, General Birney's Adjutant-General, rode up to Col. Shaw with the order to send four companies deployed as skirmishers "to attack and take the work that is firing." Colonel Shaw replied that he had orders to charge it with his regiment to which Captain Bailey answered, "Well, *now* the General directs you to send four companies, deployed as skirmishers, to take the work."
>
> Captain Weiss, when he received the order to charge, replied, "What! Take a fort with a skirmish line?" and then added, "I will try, but it can't be done."

Although the 54th Massachusetts' assault on Fort Wagner brought it glory, the price in blood was high, as shown by this roll of missing soldiers. (National Archives)

List of the Names of the Enlisted men of the 54th Regiment Mass. Vols. Missing after the assault on Ft. Wagner July 18th 1863

Capt Weiss, one of the 7th USCI's officers who commanded companies C, D, G, and K that day, described the attack in the 7th USCI's memoirs:

In a few minutes the ditch of the fort was reached. It was some six or seven feet deep and ten or twelve wide, with the excavated material sufficing for the embankments of the fort. Some 120 men and officers precipitated themselves into it, many losing their lives at its very edge. After a short breathing spell men were helped up the exterior slope of the parapet on the shoulders of others, and fifty or sixty being thus disposed an attempt was made to storm the fort. At the signal nearly all rose, but the enemy, lying securely sheltered behind the interior slope, the muzzles of their guns almost touching the storming party, received the latter with a crushing fire, sending many into the ditch below shot through the brain or breast. Several other attempts were made with like results, till at last forty or fifty of the assailants were writhing in the ditch or resting forever.

The defense having been reinforced ... it was considered impolitic to attempt anther storm, with the now greatly reduced force on hand... [With] no signs of [reinforcements] appearing it was decided to surrender, especially as the rebels had now commenced to roll lighted shells among the stormers. Seven officers, and from seventy to eighty enlisted men, delivered up their arms.

Union generals learned to value African American troops. Henry Freeman described his regiment's first experience under fire, at the Battle of Dalton, and his commanding general's reaction to it:

The fire was not heavy, but men had fallen. As coolly as if on drill, the line pushed through the briars and brush, while the main line, farther to the right, became very much broken by passing among the huts, the rebel skirmishers falling back before it. After clearing the buildings it was halted for a moment for rectification. At the command guides sprang out with inverted muskets, and the broken ranks closed on the center, though at least two men fell dead from the enemy's fire while the movement was going on. General Steedman, who commanded the Composite Division made up of units Sherman had left behind when he went to Atlanta, from his

African American troops clear Confederate troops out of rifle pits at St. James Island in February 1865. Note the white officers and NCOs. (Potter Collection)

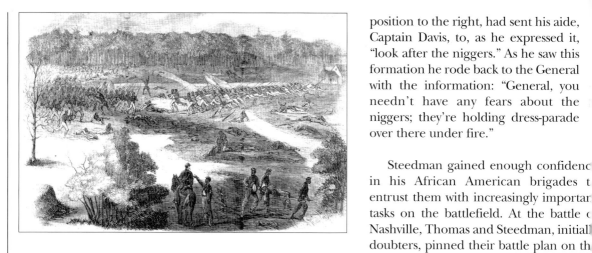

Duncan's Brigade of African American regiments attacks the Confederate line at Petersburg. (Potter Collection)

position to the right, had sent his aide, Captain Davis, to, as he expressed it, "look after the niggers." As he saw this formation he rode back to the General with the information: "General, you needn't have any fears about the niggers; they're holding dress-parade over there under fire."

Steedman gained enough confidenc in his African American brigades t entrust them with increasingly importar tasks on the battlefield. At the battle c Nashville, Thomas and Steedman, initiall doubters, pinned their battle plan on th steadiness of the African American troops, and were rewarded with decisive victory.

African American troops also gained the confidence of their whit counterparts. Thomas Morgan recalled that "The Lieutenant Colone commanding the Sixty-eighth Indiana Volunteer Infantry requested m as a personal favor to ask for the assignment of his regiment to m command, giving as a reason that he would rather fight alongside of th Fourteenth Colored, than with any other regiment."

Respect for black troops was not limited to the Army of th Cumberland. In Virginia, a *New York Herald* correspondent reported, "A Ohio soldier said to me today, 'I never saw men fight with such desperat gallantry as those negroes did. They advanced as grim and stern as deatl and when within reach of the enemy, struck about them with a pitiless vigc that was almost fearful'" (Brown).

Some whites viewed the African American troops as fearles automatons, unaware or uncaring of the odds against them. Yet mos African American troops understood the dangers associated with battle As Thomas Cole, an artilleryman who later served in the 2nd U Colored Light Artillery, and who served unofficially as a loader in white artillery regiment at the battle of Chickamauga, put it, "I never di get to where I wasn't scared when we goes into the battle" (Col Narrative).

Cole's description of the battle of Chickamauga highlighted th confusion and danger of combat, and the reaction of a typical soldier white or black:

I helps set them cannons on this Chickamauga Mountain in hiding places. I have to go with a man and wait on him and that cannon. First thing I knows, bang, bang, boom things has started and guns are shooting faster than you can think, and I looks round for the way to run. But them guns is shooting down the hill in front of me and shooting at me and over me and on both sides of me. I tries to dig a hole and get in it. All this happens right now, and first thing I knows, the man is kicking me and wanting me to help him keep that cannon loaded. Man, I didn't want no cannon, but I has to help anyway. We fought till dark ... I done told Gen. Rosecran that I wants to fight the Rebels, and he sure was letting me do it. He wasn't just letting me do it; he was *making* me do it.

Cole also provided a vivid account of his experience at Lookout Mountain and at Missionary Ridge:

They starts climbing this steep mountain and when us gets three-fourths of the way up it was foggy and you could not see no place. Everything wet and the rocks are slick and they begin fighting. I expect some shoots their own men because you couldn't see nothing, just men running and the guns roaring. Finally them Rebels fled and we gets on Lookout Mountain and takes it.

By 1864 attitudes towards African American troops had shifted dramatically since the war's outbreak. Here white soldiers cheer their black comrades as they bring in a captured Confederate cannon. (Potter Collection)

There a long range of hills leading away from Lookout Mountain, nearly to Missionary Ridge. This ridge alongside the Chickamauga River, what in the Indian name meaning "River of Death." I was in the Missionary Ridge battle. We has to come out the timber and run across a strip or opening up the hill. They sure killed lots our men when we runs across that opening. We runs for all we's worth and uses guns or anything we could. The Rebels turns and runs off and our soldiers turns the cannons round that we's capture and killed some the Rebels with their own guns.

Alexander Newton, a less reluctant warrior, frankly admitted his fears:

Many, such as myself, [were] almost afraid of my own shadow, ready to shoot at anything that made a threatening noise. I remember that I shot at the limb of a tree floating down the river, thinking it was a rebel skiff with spies. It was a sore and trying ordeal. Every soldier was in constant expectation of surprises from the Johnnies or rebels.

Fear did not prevent him from doing his duty. Newton vividly described his participation in an assault on Confederate rifle pits, following Col W. L. Ward, temporarily commanding Newton's regiment:

He brought us up double-quick to the rifle pits and the bugle sounded charge. We charged, firing, yelling, using our bayonets and our arms in the most cruel manner, but in accordance with the tactics of warfare. We were there to kill in every manner possible. We held the pits for twenty-four hours, brought the rebels to their knees, brought down their flag and unfurled the Stars and Stripes to the breezes.

Most black troops faced the challenge offered by battle. Thomas Morgan related how his men reacted to the prospect of fighting Bedford Forrest, the commander of Confederate cavalry in Tennessee, who had ed the Confederate forces at the Fort Pillow Massacre earlier in 1864:

A regiment's colors – its regimental flag – were a rallying point, and a symbol of the regiment. This flag, that of the 6th USCI, shows Liberty with a black soldier, and bears the motto "Freedom for All." (Library of Congress, Prints and Photographs Division)

At length the enemy in strong force, with banners flying, bore down towards us in full sight, apparently bent on mischief. Pointing to the advancing column I said, as I passed along the line: "Boys, it looks very much like fight. Keep cool, do your duty." They seemed full of glee, and replied with great enthusiasm: "Colonel, they can't whip us; they never get the ole Fourteenth out of here, never." "Never drives us away without a mighty lot of dead men."

Gen Nathan Bedford Forrest, in this case, proved to b more intimidated than Morgan's men, "When Forre: learned that Rousseau was reinforced by infantry, he di not stop to ask about the color of skin, but after testing ou line, and finding it unyielding, turned to the east concluded Morgan.

Battle was not without risks. Chief among them wer injury and capture. Civil War firearms produce devastating wounds. Despite this, African American soldiers ofte ignored injuries. Albert Jones described his reaction to being wounded "One day when I was fighting, the rebels shot at me, and they sent bullet through my hand. I was lucky not to be killed. But that didn't sto me. I had it bandaged and kept on fighting" (Jones Narrative).

Morgan related an incident involving a soldier wounded at Nashvill "One private soldier in Company B, who had taken a position in a tre as a sharpshooter, had his right arm broken by a ball. Captain Romey said to him: 'You would better come down from there, go to the rea and find the surgeon.' 'Oh, no, Captain,' was his reply, 'I can fire wit my left arm,' and so he did."

Those who did seek medical attention clung to their weapor tenaciously. Solon Carter told about a surgeon awakened at daybrea following a battle by a wounded soldier.

The caller was a colored soldier who had been shot through the right lung the previous afternoon, the bullet passing through his body. The man had followed the retreating column through mud and rain for ten miles, bringing his gun and equipments with him.

Surgeon Barns dressed the wound and placed him in charge of the ambulance corps. Asked why he had brought his gun, the brave fellow replied that he "Didn't care to be in those parts without something to protect hisself."

Many put their faith in God to protect them. "I never have bee wounded. My clothes have been cut off me by bullets, but the Lord key them off my back, I guess," stated Richard Slaughter of the 19th USC in an interview.

Alexander Newton took a more personal view of Divine Interventio

I remember a twenty-pound cannon ball coming towards me, I could see it distinctly through the smoke. I said quickly, "Lord, you promised that a thousand should fall at my side, but that it should not come nigh me." It was quick praying, quick thinking, quick coming; but when the ball was within about three feet of me it struck the ground and bounded over my head.

Another risk faced by African American troops was capture. The Confederacy never officially recognized them as legal combatants. At Milliken's Bend captured blacks were killed out of hand or claimed as slaves, at the whim of their owners. Two white officers and NCOs captured there were executed for fomenting slave insurrection. Formal executions of captured USCT personnel ended after Grant threatened to hang captured Confederates in reprisal. Unsanctioned murders continued throughout the war, however, including a massacre of African American troops captured at Fort Pillow in April 1864.

As Alexander Newton related, threats failed to force blacks off the battlefield.

> We were told by the enemy that if we were captured our tongues would be cut out, or we would be starved to death; that there would be no exchange of prisoners in our case. So this was a rather fearful inspiration, but it served its purpose, of causing us to fight to the best of our ability; for we really feared that in case we were captured that such barbarities might be administered to us.

Every battle left a fearful toll, whether the African American troops won or lost. Cole related the aftermath of the battle of Missionary Ridge. It was:

> the last one I was in and I was sure glad, for I never seed the like of dead and wounded men. We picks them up, the Rebels like the Unions, and doctors them the best we could. When I seed all that suffering, I hopes I never live to see another war... I just couldn't stand to see all them men laying there dying and hollering, and begging for help and a drink of water, and blood everywheres you looks. Killing hogs back on the plantation didn't bother me none, but this was different.

Alexander Newton had a similar reaction after an assault at Petersburg:

> I came on my rounds, bringing refreshments and stopped where the surgeons were at work. I shall never forget the fearful sight that met my eyes. There were arms and legs piled up like hogs' feet in a butcher shop. The dead and dying were strewn over the battlefield for five miles.

Susie King Taylor told of the aftermath of a bloody action fought by the 33rd USCI:

> About four o'clock, July 2, the charge was made. The firing could be plainly heard in camp. I hastened down to the landing and remained there until eight o'clock that morning. When the wounded arrived, or rather began to arrive the first one they

Alexander H. Newton, in full dress uniform while he was quartermaster sergeant for the 29th Connecticut Infantry (Colored). Note the tasseled sash and NCO sword. Though of poor quality, this is the only known picture of one of the black participants quoted in this book. (Author's collection)

brought in was Samuel Anderson of our company. He was badly wounded. Then others of our boys, some with their legs off, arm gone, foot off, and wounds of all kinds imaginable.

Medical services were crude during the Civil War, more so fo African American troops. Often, as Taylor explained, initial treatmen for the wounded was little more than crude first aid:

It seems strange how our aversion to seeing suffering is overcome in war, – how we are able to see the most sickening sights, such as men with their limbs blown off and mangled by the deadly shells, without a shudder; and instead of turning away, how we hurry to assist in alleviating their pain, bind up their wounds, and press cool water to their parched lips, with feelings only of sympathy and pity.

Sometimes, as Esther Hill Hawks recorded in her diary, a flood c casualties overwhelmed available medical services, delaying medica treatment:

What a terrible sight it was! It was 36 hours since the awful struggle at Fort Wagner, and nothing had been done for them. We had no beds, and no means even of building a fire, but the colored people came promptly to our aid, and almost before we knew what we needed they brought us buckets full of nice broth and gruels, pitchers of lemonade, fruits, cakes, vegetables; indeed everything needed for the immediate wants of the men was furnished... Everything for our immediate wants was furnished, and in 24 hours the poor fellows were lying with clean clothes and dressed wounds in comfortable beds.

Throughout the war, the Union expanded its hospital system. Africa American troops who reached a hospital received medical treatment o a par with that given to white troops, and were kept as long as wa

The battle of the Crater resulted in one of the Civil War's biggest slaughters of African American troops. Here the African American regiments plunge into the crater formed by an underground mine in an effort to rescue the white regiments sent in with the first wave. (Author's collection)

quired for their recovery. Charles Gabriel Anderson, who enlisted in the 56th USCI, spent over a year in a hospital, and was discharged the year after the war ended, in 1866.

The staff sometimes had an uphill struggle to get former slaves to accept proper medical treatment. Hawks noted that a:

> great difficulty to be overcome was to get them to sleep between sheets. They stared aghast on being told to get in between such immaculate whiteness... when those who were able made their beds, the sheets of some were carefully folded and lain on the outside of their beds, while others spread them over the blankets, and got into bed upon the bare mattress.

To these men, most former slaves, clean, white sheets were an unimaginable luxury.

AFTERMATH

When the war ended, I goes back to my master, and he treated me like his brother. Guess he was scared of me, because I had so much ammunition with me.

(Albert Jones, Co K, 1st Colored Cavalry [Jones Narrative])

Was their service worth it for the blacks who fought in the United States Army during the Civil War? George Grant thought it was. Many times after the war he would tell his daughter, Omelia Thomas, "I am part of the cause that you are free" (Thomas Narrative). Charles H. Anderson was less impressed with freedom. "After the war I was free. But it didn't make much difference to me. I had to work for myself instead of somebody else" (Anderson Narrative).

Two soldiers pose with rifles outside a deserted house. (Library of Congress, Prints and Photographs Division)

Not every black soldier benefited from service. John Pope spok
bitterly about how his father, Gus Pope, was treated: "He served in the wa
three years and never came home. He served in the 63rd Regimen
Infantry of the Yankee Army. He died right at the surrender... My fathe
was promised $300.00 bounty and 160 acres of land... No he never go
nary penny nor nary acre of land. We ain't got nothing" (Pope Narrative)

Some veterans of the USCT joined the Regular Army after the wa
becoming part of the famed "Buffalo Soldiers." There, they had onc
again to prove their worth, as the frontier posts were garrisoned b
"galvanized Yankees" – Confederate prisoners of war who gained releas
by joining the Union Army to serve in the West. As to the fates o
individual USCT soldiers quoted in this book:

Charles Gabriel Anderson (56th USCI) became a barber, a carriag
driver, and a window washer.

Charles H. Anderson (122nd USCI) worked for the C&O Railroa
for 30 years, "bossing" a track gang.

Peter Bruner became one of the first black employees of Miami o
Ohio University, eventually retiring with a pension.

Henry H. Buttler went to college, became an engineer after the wa
and later spent 22 years as an educator.

William Baltimore (4th USCHA), Thomas Cole (1st USCLA), Willian
Emmons (117th USCI), George Grant (78th USCI), Albert Jones (1s
USCC), and James Spikes (55th USCI) returned to farming. All lived int
their 80s and 90s.

John Eubanks worked at a lumberyard after the war.

James Henry Gooding (54th Massachusetts) was badly wounded an
captured defending the colors at Olustee. He died at Andersonvill
Prison in 1864.

Charles Hubbard (6th USCI) died at Petersburg.

Alexander Newton (29th Connecticut Volunteers) was discharged i
1865, returned to his store, felt the calling of religion, and became
minister. He wrote his memoirs in 1910.

Prince Rivers (1st South Carolina and 33rd USCI) entered politic
and was elected to South Carolina's Reconstruction government.

Richard Slaughter (19th USCI) survived th
shambles at the Crater, and worked as an oysterma
and fisherman in Hampton, Virginia, for over 40 year
after his discharge.

Isaac Stokeley's fate is unknown.

Susie King Taylor became a schoolteacher after th
war, and later retired to Massachusetts, where, with th
aid of the former officers of the 33rd USCI, sh
published her memoirs, now considered a classic o
Civil War literature.

As these black men in blue uniforms grew olde
many wrote their memoirs, but memories of thei
accomplishments faded. Between 1925 and 1950, man
historians ignored their contributions.

Despite this, the USCT veterans benefited from thei
service. Army service gave veterans both organizationa
and leadership skills. Moreover, as Albert Jones realized
it provided a nucleus of black men schooled in wa

A USCT cavalry sergeant (third in line), probably from the 4th USCC regiment, savors one of the fruits of his efforts in the USCT. He is about to cast his vote for the first time in his life. (Library of Congress, Prints and Photographs Division)

56

Immediately after the Civil War, blacks had rights that they would not regain until after World War II. They could vote, and in many cases could and did run for public office.

There was some erosion of these rights in the 1870s, but not until Reconstruction ended and these veterans started growing old, in the 1880s, did the South begin imposing large numbers of laws limiting the rights of blacks.

Even then, those who had served in the USCT did better than those who had not. Life was hard for all blacks at the end of the 19th century, but it was harder for non-veterans. Veterans were eligible for pensions. Henry Buttler and his wife, Lucia, retired on the $75/month pension he received. James Spikes was 91 when he told an interviewer, "The government gives me a pension now cause I was a soldier. It comes in right nice – it does that" (Spikes Narrative).

Some veterans were cheated of their pensions, but many received them. As William Baltimore, who served in the 4th USCHA Regiment, related to an interviewer, "It was a lucky day when the Yankees gets me. If they hadn't I don't know what'd become of me. After I went blind, I had hard times. Some of my white friends dug up my record with the Yankees and got me a pension. Now I am sitting pretty for the rest of my life" (Baltimore Narrative).

An infantry frock coat, now an exhibit at the Buffalo Soldiers National Museum, is typical of the uniforms issued to colored troops. (Author's photograph)

MUSEUMS AND REENACTMENT

There are several museums on the black contribution to the Civil War. The African American Civil War Memorial Freedom Foundation and Museum at 1200 U Street N.W., Washington, DC 20009, is a national museum dedicated to the service of the USCT during the American Civil War. The museum is open Monday to Friday from 10am to 5pm, and Saturday 10am to 2pm. You can get more information at the museum's website: *http://www.afroamcivilwar.org*.

Another good African American military history museum is the Buffalo Soldiers National Museum, at 834 Southmore, Houston, TX

At the war's end, most of the African American regiments were mustered out, and sent home. Here the troops of the 54th USCI greet their wives and children upon their discharge. USCT soldiers, like their white counterparts, were allowed to keep their personal weapons. (Library of Congress, Prints and Photographs Division)

77004. Privately owned, it has a more general focus, covering the military activities of African Americans in the United States from the Revolution through to today's "War on Terror." This museum is open Monday to Friday 10am to 5pm, Saturday 10am to 4pm. Its website is *http://www.buffalosoldiermuseum.com.*

On the web, one really outstanding resource for those interested in the USCT is the United States Colored Troops' website (*http://www.lwfaam. net/cw*), compiled by Bennie J. McRae, Jr.

Several groups reenact the service of the USCT soldiers. The United States Colored Troops Living History Association (*http:// www.usctlha.org*) is a national organization with 13 different "regiments" throughout the United States.

The 54th Massachusetts and 1st South Carolina (later the 33rd USCI) are two units popular with reenactors. There are several groups of 54th Massachusetts reenactors. 54th. Mass. Volunteer Infantry, Co. operates out of Charleston, SC. Its website is *http://www.awod. com/cwchas/54ma.html.* Co. B is in Washington DC. Its website is *http://www.54thmass.org/54about.html.* The 1st US South Carolina maintains a web page at *http://www.awod.com/cwchas/1sc.html.*

Several battlefield parks also have annual reenactments of battles involving black troops. The most notable is the Olustee Battlefield in Florida, which annually reenacts that battle. Its web page is *http://extlab1.entnem.ufl.edu/olustee/index.html.*

Another group of reenactors is associated with Camp Nelson, Kentucky, one of the main training camps for the US Colored Troops. Camp Nelson is now a Heritage Park, with reenacting groups representing the 12th United States Colored Heavy Artillery, 5th United States Colored Cavalry, and 5th United States Colored Infantry, all units that trained at Camp Nelson. The Camp Nelson website is *http://www.campnelson.org/home.htm.*

The band of the 107th USCI. Although the bandsmen are all black, the bandmaster (left) is a white NCO. (Library of Congress, Prints and Photographs Division)

BIBLIOGRAPHY

Books

Ayers, James T., *The Diary of James T. Ayers, Civil War Recruiter*, printed by authority of the State of Illinois, Springfield, IL (1947, rev. edn Louisiana State University Press, 1999)

Brown, William Wells, *The Negro in the American Rebellion; his Heroism and his Fidelity*, Lee and Shepard, Boston (1867, rev. edn Ohio University Press, 2003)

Bruner, Peter, *A Slave's Adventures Toward Freedom; not Fiction, but the True Story of a Struggle*, Oxford, OH (1910)

Califf, Joseph M., *Record of the Services of the Seventh Regiment, U.S. Colored Troops*, E. L. Freeman & Co., Providence, RI (1878)

Chenery, William H., *The Fourteenth Regiment Rhode Island Heavy Artillery (Colored) in the War to Preserve the Union, 1861–1865*, Snow & Farnham, Providence, RI (1898)

Cimprich, John, *Fort Pillow, a Civil War Massacre, and Public Memory*, Louisiana State University Press, Baton Rouge (2005)

Clark, Peter H., *The Black Brigade of Cincinnati; Being a Report of its Labors and a Muster-roll of its Members; Together with Various Orders, Speeches, etc., Relating to it*, J. B. Boyd, Cincinnati (1864)

Cornish, Dudley Taylor, *The Sable Arm; Negro Troops in the Union Army, 1861–1865*, Longmans, Green, New York (1956, rev. edn, University Press of Kansas, 1987)

— *Kansas Negro Regiments in the Civil War*, State of Kansas Commission on Civil Rights, Topeka, KS (1969)

Dyer, Frederick H., *A Compendium of the War of the Rebellion, Compiled and Arranged from Official Records of the Federal and Confederate Armies, Reports of the Adjutant Generals of the Several States, the Army Registers and Other Reliable Documents and Sources in 3 Volumes*, Dyer Publishing Co., Des Moines, IA (1908)

Emilio, Luis F., *History of the Fifty-fourth Regiment of Massachusetts Volunteer Infantry, 1863–1865*, The Boston Book Company, Boston (1894) (Modern reprints use the title *A Brave Black Regiment*)

Gladstone, William A., *United States Colored Troops, 1863–1867*, Thomas Publications, Gettysburg, PA (1990)

Gooding, James Henry (ed. Virginia M. Adams), *On the Altar of Freedom: a Black Soldier's Civil War Letters from the Front*, Warner Books, New York (1992)

Hawks, Esther Hill, *A Woman Doctor's Civil War: Esther Hill Hawks' Diary, Edited with a Foreword by Gerald Schwartz*, University of South Carolina Press, Columbia, SC (1992)

Higginson, Thomas Wentworth, *Army Life in a Black Regiment*, Fields, Osgood & Co., Boston (1870)

Hollandsworth, James G. Jr., *The Louisiana Native Guards: the Black Military Experience During the Civil War*, Louisiana State University Press, Baton Rouge (1995)

Knox, Thomas Wallace, *Camp-Fire and Cotton-Field: Southern Adventure in Time of War*, Blelock and Company, New York (1865)

McMurray, John, *Recollections of a Colored Troop*, The McMurray Company, Brookville, PA (1994)

Newton, Alexander H., *Out of the Briars: an Autobiography and Sketch of the Twenty-ninth Regiment, Connecticut Volunteers*, The A.M.E. Book Concern, Philadelphia (1910)

Post, Lydia Minturn (ed.), *Soldiers' Letters from Camp, Battle-Field, and Prison*, Bunce and Huntington, New York (1865)

Redkey, Edwin S. (ed.), *A Grand Army of Black Men: Letters from African American Soldiers in the Union Army, 1861–1865*, Cambridge University Press, New York (1992)

Shaffer, Donald R., *After the Glory, The Struggles of Black Civil War Veterans*, University Press of Kansas, Lawrence (2004)

Smith, John David (ed.), *Black Soldiers in Blue: African American Troops in the Civil War Era*, University of North Carolina Press, Chapel Hill (2002)

Taylor, Susie King, *Reminiscences of my Life in Camp: a Black Woman's Civil War Memoirs*, Boston, published by the author (1902, rev. edn, University of Georgia Press, 2006)

Trudeau, Noah Andre, *Like Men of War: Black Troops in the Civil War, 1862–1865*, Little, Brown, Boston (1998)

Urwin, Gregory A. W. (ed.), *Black Flag over Dixie: Racial Atrocities and Reprisals in the Civil War*, Southern Illinois University Press, Carbondale (2004)

US Congress Joint Committee on the Conduct of the War, *Fort Pillow Massacre*, Washington, DC (1864)

US War Dept, *The War of the Rebellion: a Compilation*

of the Official Records of the Union and Confederate Armies. 128v. GPO, Washington, DC (1880–1901)

Washington, Versalle F., *Eagles on their Buttons*, University of Missouri Press, Columbia, MO (1984)

Weaver, C. P. (ed.), *Thank God my Regiment an African One: the Civil War Diary of Colonel Nathan W. Daniels*, Louisiana State University Press, Baton Rouge (1998)

Williams, George W., *A History of the Negro Troops in the War of the Rebellion 1861–1865*, Harper & Brothers, New York (1888)

Wilson, Joseph T., *The Black Phalanx*, American Publishing Company, Hartford, CT (1890)

Articles and pamphlets

Addeman, J. M., Capt, "Reminiscences of Two Years with the Colored Troops," *Personal Narratives of the Events in the War of the Rebellion, Being Papers Read Before the Rhode Island Soldiers and Sailors Historical Society, Volume II*, published by the Society, Providence, RI (1894)

Armstrong, William H., Lt, "The Negro as a Soldier," *War Papers, Read Before the Indiana Commandery, Military Order of the Loyal Legion of the United States, Volume 1*, The Commandery, Indianapolis (1898)

Baird, J. M., Lt Col, 32nd USCT, "The 32nd Regiment U.S.C.T at the Battle of Honey Hill," 159 High Street, Boston, MA (1889)

Carter, Solon A., Bvt Lt Col, USV, "Fourteen Months' Service with Colored Troops," *Civil War Papers, Read Before the Commandery of the State of Massachusetts, Military Order of the Loyal Legion of the United States, Volume 1*, The Commandery, Boston (1900)

Connor, Selden, "The Colored Troops," *War Papers, Read Before the Commandery of the State of Maine, Military Order of the Loyal Legion of the United States, Volume 1*, Lefavor-Tower Company, Portland, ME (1908)

Freeman, Henry V., Capt, 12th Inf. USCT, "A Colored Brigade in the Campaign and Battle of Nashville," *Military Essays and Recollections Volume II*, A. C. McClurg and Co., Chicago (1894)

Furness, William Eliot, Maj and Judge Advocate, USV, "The Negro as a Soldier," *Military Essays and Recollections, Volume II*, A. C. McClurg and Co., Chicago (1894)

Matson, Dan, "The Colored Man in the Civil War," *War Sketches and Incidents as Related by the Companions of the Iowa Commandery, Military Order of the Loyal Legion of the United States Volume II*, Des Moines, IA (1898)

Morgan, Thomas J., "Reminiscences of Service with the Colored Troops in the Army of the Cumberland, 1863–65," *Personal Narratives of the Events in the War of the Rebellion, Being Papers Read Before the Rhode Island Soldiers and Sailors Historical Society, Volume V*, published by the Society, Providence, RI (1885)

Norton, Henry Allyn, Capt and Bvt Maj, 92nd Illinois USV, "Colored Troops In The War Of The Rebellion," *Glimpses of the Nation's Struggle, Fifth Series*, Review Publishing Co., St Paul, MN (1903)

Parker, W. Thornton, MD, "The Evolution of the Colored Soldier," *The North American Review* Vol. CLXVIII, New York (1899)

Perkins, Frances Beecher, "Two Years with a Colored Regiment, a Woman's Experience," *New England Magazine*, Boston, MA, vol. 1 (September 1897–February 1898)

Rickard, James H., "Services with Colored Troops in Burnside's Corps," *Personal Narratives of the Events in the War of the Rebellion, Being Papers Read Before the Rhode Island Soldiers and Sailors Historical Society, Volume VIII*, published by the Society, Providence, RI (1894)

Romeyn, Henry, "With Colored Troops in the Army of the Cumberland," *War Papers No 51*, MOLLUS, Commandery of the District of Columbia (January 6, 1904)

Sherman, George R., "The Negro as a Soldier," *Personal Narratives of the Events in the War of the Rebellion, Being Papers Read Before the Rhode Island Soldiers and Sailors Historical Society, Volume 2*, published by the Society, Providence, RI (1913)

Simonton, Edwin, Capt, 1st US Colored Infantry, Bvt Lt Col, USV, "The Campaign up the James River to Petersburg," *Glimpses of the Nation's Struggle, Fifth Series*, Review Publishing Co., St Paul, MN (1903)

Sutherland, George E., Capt, 13th USCT, "The Negro in the Late War," *War Papers, Being Papers Read before the Commandery of the State of Wisconsin, Military Order of the Loyal Legion of the United States, Volume 1* (April 4, 1888)

Trowbridge, Charles Tyler, Lt Col, 33rd USCI, "Six Months in the Freedmen's Bureau with a Colored Regiment," *Glimpses of the Nation's Struggle, Sixth Series*, Aug. Davis, Publisher, Minneapolis, MN (1909)

Blacks often served as teamsters and pioneers for the Union Army. Although these men were not armed, they shared the same risks as African American soldiers. (Potter Collection)

Two black soldiers sit by a bombproof shelter at Dutch Gap during the siege of Petersburg. (Library of Congress, Prints and Photographs Division)

Web resources

Bruner, Jacob, Jacob Bruner Letters (unpublished collection, 1863) *http://memory.loc.gov/ammem/award97/ohshtml/aaeohome.html*, keywords "Jacob Bruner"

Civil War Soldiers and Sailors System, *http://www.itd.nps.gov/cwss/index.html*, National Park Service – lists information about units, individual soldiers, and battles

Omenhausser, John Jacob, *Point Lookout Album* (unpublished collection of sketches made at Point Lookout, MD, by a POW, 1864), now in the New York Historical Society, *http://memory.loc.gov/ammem/ndlpcoop/nhihtml/cwnyhshome.html*, keywords: "Omenausser, Point Lookout Album"

Prints and Photographs Online Catalog (PPOC), *http://www.loc.gov/rr/print/catalog.html*, United States Library of Congress

Slave Narratives, Federal Writers' Project, Multiformat 1936–1938, United States Library of Congress (*http://memory.loc.gov/ammem/snhtml/snhome.html*)

COLOR PLATE COMMENTARY

A: PRIVATE, 54TH MASSACHUSETTS, 1863

The 54th Massachusetts (Colored) was one of the first African American regiments raised, and one of only four African American regiments which remained in commission until the end of the Civil War to retain a state designation (the 55th Massachusetts and 29th Connecticut Infantry regiments and the 5th Massachusetts Colored Cavalry were the others). Famed for its attack on Battery Wagner in July 1863, it fought at other major battles including Olustee. It has been the subject of many books, and the movie *Glory*.

An elite unit, it was made up of free, mostly educated blacks from throughout the Northern states. Among those enlisting were both sons of Frederick Douglass, James Gooding (a whaler who was also a published author), and George Stephens, a reporter and rights activist. Many enlisted not just seeking freedom for their enslaved brethren, but as a first step in achieving legal equality with whites.

This plate shows the appearance of a typical private of the regiment, prior to its departure to Charleston (1). Like most African American regiments, the 54th was well equipped. The clothing was of good quality, the equipment excellent, and the weapons issued – in this case the 1853 Enfield (2) –

first class. Typical of USCT – when not overloaded with fatigue duties – this soldier maintains his kit and uniform in top condition as a matter of pride. Shown here are external (3) and internal (4) views of a cartridge.

B: TRAINING VIGNETTES

Camp Nelson, Kentucky, was a major training post for USCT soldiers, serving as a depot for blacks from Kentucky, Tennessee, and Ohio. Only Camp William Penn, in Philadelphia, exceeded its output of regiments. This plate shows the cycle experienced by USCT soldiers as they trained. A recruiter, usually one of the officers in a regiment under formation, would come to camp with his latest crop of volunteers. Peter Bruner wrote in his memoirs of the party-like atmosphere in his group: "The next morning about five o'clock I got up and started for Camp Nelson... I came upon sixteen colored fellows who were on their way to Camp Nelson and of course I did not get lonesome."

At the camp, recruits were formed into companies. "Immediately upon our arrival here on Wednesday afternoon, we marched to the barracks, where we found a nice warm fire and a good supper in readiness for us. During the evening the

Blacks flock to a recruiting office. (Author's collection)

men were all supplied with uniforms, and now they are looking quite like soldiers," wrote James Gooding of his arrival at a training camp. Initially, as shown in the top scene, drill would be pretty rough, as the men practiced in the yard in front of the barracks at Camp Nelson, but soon the men would come together, and work as a team, as shown at the bottom. At that point, they would be ready to fight.

C: AN INTRODUCTION TO ONE'S KIT

It must have seemed miraculous that the Army gave a man in the USCT the clothes and tools to be a soldier for free. A soldier's kit was worth $70 to $100 – a fortune to a man who previously had not even owned the clothes on his back. Being told it was his to keep engendered pride of possession and a desire to maintain his property in top condition. Henry Freeman, a white officer in an African American regiment, noted that his men "were pleased with their guns, pleased with their uniforms, and impressed with their own importance as soldiers."

The men in his company would often introduce a new recruit in an established unit to his kit. Often, in addition to his NCO, in this case a corporal, he would be assigned an experienced private, with the willingness to work with the new recruit. He would be shown what the kit consisted of, and how to pack and store the elements that made it up. In this case, our new private has joined one of the 13 heavy artillery regiments in the USCT. These units generally garrisoned a fort, such as those controlling travel on the Mississippi. They lived in permanent barracks, and tended to have more lavish

An African American soldier posting guard at an artillery park. (Library of Congress, Prints and Photographs Division)

kits than troops in campaigning infantry or cavalry regiments. Our soldier has a shell jacket, as well as the sack coat and frock, an additional blanket, and more spare clothes.

D: CAPTURE OF OVERTON'S HILL

African American troops played a key role in the critical Union victory at Nashville in December 1864. They were assigned to Steedman's Division, a provisional force of units left behind when Sherman marched from Atlanta, which was stationed on the Union left. On the morning of battle, December 15, the African American troops were to make a demonstration against the Confederates fortified on Overton's Hill. The troops let their enthusiasm run away with them. Instead of feigning an attack, they charged and almost carried the hill. The attack convinced the Confederates to shift their reserves to that flank. They were caught flat-footed when the main Union attack hit their right in the early afternoon.

Hearing word that the army was attacking, the previously repulsed African American regiments launched a second attack on the reinforced Overton's Hill. Confederate troops, shaken by word that their left was folding, broke and ran just before the wave of black soldiers reached the breastworks. They left several stands of regimental colors and the artillery emplaced there.

It was bitterly cold. Union troops fought wearing their greatcoats, carrying cartridge boxes and canteens. Packs and haversacks were left behind. The enemy defenses, built in the freezing weather of the previous days, consisted of felled trees and piled rock. The Confederates holding the hill were cold, ill fed, and poorly clothed. Rather than the smart uniforms of the Union soldiers, they were clad in the rags that had been their issue clothing and whatever they could scavenge from the battlefield.

E: LIFE IN THE USCT

Off duty, African American troops tended to be a temperate lot. Capt George Sutherland observed there "was less drunkenness, and less profanity ... than among white troops" (Sutherland, "The Negro in the Late War"). Instead, these soldiers tended to spend their free time tending their equipment or learning. Literate soldiers, generally the sergeants, would teach others to read. George O'Meal wrote, "In one corner you would see a grown-up man trying to teach a drummer-boy to write; in another you would see a man about thirty, trying to learn his letters without a teacher" (Post).

A major pastime was religion. "A Negro soldiers' camp at night was sure to be the scene of some religious observance," stated Capt Sutherland. Religion was one of the few comforts allowed slaves, and they carried their belief into camp. Services were performed out in the open air, with a self-appointed lay preacher leading them, often mixing military allusions into a sermon. Sutherland described how "... the preacher rises and pours forth his wild exhortation, 'You must follow the heavenly flag, and shoot with the heavenly gun.'"

Black troops also took their responsibilities seriously when on duty. One task many black troops were used for was guarding Confederate prisoners. The soldier in the inset is shown on guard duty at Elmira Prison in New York, beginning a long night shift. John Whipple, a white guard at Elmira, noted that "the most trustworthy and reliable guards we have at this place are negroes" (Post).

THE BATTLE OF HONEY SPRINGS

n the same day that the 54th Massachusetts was being
pulsed at Battery Wagner, another African American
giment, the 1st Kansas Infantry (Colored), was contributing
the greatest Union victory of the Trans-Mississippi Theater,
Honey Springs in the Indian Territory. The 1st Kansas
olored) was probably the best-trained unit on either side.
aised in late 1862 from runaway slaves from Missouri, owing
politics and a mistrust of the reliability of blacks it trained
til committed to service in early summer 1863.

In the center of the Union line, exposed to enemy fire, the
en were ordered to lie down in the tall grass. The officers
mained standing to direct the battle. Several were injured.
hen a Union Indian Cavalry regiment in reserve behind their
e began redeploying, the Confederates assumed the
nion was retreating. Anxious to destroy the Yankees, the
onfederates, a mixed force of Texas and Confederate
dian cavalry regiments, charged.

As the charge began, the 1st Kansas, on orders from their
ficers, stood. They fired three volleys in quick succession,
redding the charging cavalry. The plate depicts the 1st
ansas (Colored) as they rose from the grass. The color
ard, a picked force of NCOs that guarded the regimental
lors, can be seen to the left. The flags shown still exist and
e on display in the Kansas State Capitol, with many more
ttle honors than they had on July 17, 1863.

THE FORT PILLOW MASSACRE

rican American troops faced the same hazards of disease
battlefield injury as the white troops, but they recognized
e reality that Confederate troops hated taking black troops
isoner. A Confederate force led by Bedford Forrest took the
eakly held Fort Pillow, manned by a white cavalry regiment
d a black artillery regiment, both under strength. After the
rt surrendered, the Confederates entered the main part of
e fort and slaughtered individual members of the garrison
they attempted to surrender. Of 262 African Americans in
e garrison only 62 survived.

One survivor, Jacob Thompson, a black cook, testified
fore a Congressional committee that investigated the
assacre. He testified that Confederate soldiers "just called
em [garrison members] out like dogs, and shot them
wn... They nailed some black sergeants to the logs and
t the logs on fire" (Joint Committee on the Conduct of the
ar, Fort Pillow Massacre).

The Union soldiers fled downhill to the river. Some, like
ompson – as shown in the plate – found boats and
caped downriver. The rest? In Thompson's words, the

njamin Butler issued this medal to the African American
ops under his command in the Army of the James. It was
e only medal exclusively issued to blacks.
uthor's collection)

Charleston was considered by the Union to be the cradle
of the revolution. The 55th Massachusetts is pictured
marching through the city after its capture. (Library
of Congress, Prints and Photographs Division)

Confederates "called them out from under the hill, and shot
them down. They would call out a white man and shoot him
down, and call out a colored man and shoot him down; do it
just as fast as they could make their guns go off" (Joint
Committee).

Forrest abandoned Fort Pillow the next morning. The
Union retook the fort. The relieving force, a white infantry
unit, buried the dead – white and black – in a mass grave
using the dry moat next to the earthen fort's parapet, as
shown in the inset. As a warning of what could happen if
African American troops surrendered, and as a call for
vengeance, "Remember Fort Pillow!" was the rallying cry for
the USCT for the rest of the Civil War.

H: GARRISON DUTY: USCT SERGEANT
MAJOR AT CHARLESTON, 1865

USCT units provided occupation troops after the war's end.
It was not duty that sprang from the love of the local
population. Lt Col Charles Trowbridge described a typical
reception when the 33rd USCI occupied a town in South
Carolina: "When we came in sight of the town where we were
to make our headquarters we were met by a committee of
the citizens who implored me 'not to bring them niggers into
their town.' ... I told them that these men were not 'niggers'
but United States soldiers, and I should march into the town
and quarter my troops in the Court House, the length of time
they would to depend entirely upon the conduct of the
townspeople towards the men and their officers."

For the occupation troops, it was an opportunity to show
that they could carry out their duties as smartly as any white
Confederate unit. This was especially true for units like the
35th USCI Regiment, which had been formed from escaped
slaves in North Carolina. The sergeant major, shown here in a
brief pause from walking his rounds in Charleston Harbor, can
be seen to take great satisfaction from his uniform and from
his status as the senior NCO in a combat regiment, but most
of all from an opportunity to garrison the rebellion's cradle.
Four years ago he may have been another slave carting goods
on Battery Street. Four years from now, he may be another
black laborer in Charleston. But today, the "bottom rail" is
on top.

INDEX